A Beginner's Guide to READING THE BIBLE

A Beginner's Guide to READING THE BIBLE

Elmer Towns

SERVANT PUBLICATIONS
ANN ARBOR, MICHIGAN

Vine Books is an imprint of Servant Publications especially designed to serve evangelical Christians.

Published by Servant Publications
P.O. Box 8617
Ann Arbor, Michigan 48107

Cover design by Alan Furst, Inc., Minneapolis, Minn.

01 02 03 04 10 9 8 7 6 5 4 3 2 1

Printed in the United States of America
ISBN 1-56955-238-X

Library of Congress Cataloging-in-Publication Data

Towns, elmer L.
A beginner's guide to reading the Bible / Elmer Towns.
p. cm.
Includes bibliographical references.
ISBN 1-56955-238-X
1. Bible—Reading. I. Title.
BS617 .T69 2001
220.6'1—dc21

2001002922

Contents

Dear Reader:

I have written this book to help you read the Bible. You might be puzzled by this statement. You might think that since you already know how to read a book, you can read the Bible. It's true you can read it like any other book because the Bible was written by authors and it is made up of normal words, sentences, paragraphs, and chapters. On the other hand, you must read the Bible differently than any other book. The Bible is God's book. It was written in a special way with a special message.

Even though the Bible looks like other books, it's unique because it tells the true story about God, different from what other books say about God. The Bible is a *revelation,* which means God has revealed himself to us in the pages of the Bible. We have not been left to imagine what God is like, nor may we create any new theories about what he is like. Other religions have holy books that describe what their leaders think God is like; our God revealed himself to us in revelation through the Bible.

Also, the Bible was written in a unique way. "Holy men of God wrote as they were moved by the Holy Spirit" (2 Peter 1:21, author's translation). That means that God's Spirit moved human authors to write the Bible. When you thumb through the pages of the Bible, you are looking at the message that God has put there for you to know.

"All scripture is given by inspiration of God" (2 Timothy 3:16). The word *inspiration* means "God breathed." God breathed on the authors as they were writing the Bible. Take a deep breath and then exhale. You can feel it: your breath is your life. When God breathed on the Bible authors, he put his life into the words of Scripture (the words *spirit* and *life* are the same). This means the Bible writers used ordinary words, but filled them with the life of God, the Spirit of God. Therefore, when you read the message of the Bible, you're receiving both the message of God and the life of God in your heart. I've written this book to help prepare you spiritually to discover the life of God—eternal life—as you read the Bible.

Let's return to the other idea, that the Bible is an ordinary book. When you read the Bible, you do the same thing as when you read the newspaper, the television listings, or a memo at work. Both secular reading and Bible reading involve recognizing words and getting information from words. Therefore when you read the Bible, you must know the meaning of its words to find out what the message is saying.

While the Bible has a supernatural message, you will find within it the styles of other literature—stories, poetry, biographies, history, and family trees. As you read, you will learn about God from the stories and you will feel God's passion from the poetry. The biographies will tell you how people lived with God and history will show you how God was working behind the scenes. These natural things will tell you about a supernatural God.

One more note: If you read the Bible at a superficial level, you will get a superficial understanding of what God says. If you read the Bible analytically, you will get analytical results. If you look for evidence of a certain idea, you'll likely find it and not much else. You will get out of Bible reading what you put into it.

You're about to embark on a wonderful adventure. You'll be reading about people like yourself. You'll see how God called one man—Abraham—and from him came the nation Israel. Since God is an honest author, the sins of Abraham and Abraham's children are recorded. Why does God include these embarrassing faults? Because as people attempted to live for God, none were perfect (just as you and I are not perfect). You'll cheer Israel's victories and weep at its defeats—and, one hopes, learn from them how to be an overcomer. You'll read of prophets who spoke for God and of kings and queens who ruled for God. You'll meet courageous people who fought for God and some who died for God. You'll hear stories of shepherds, teachers, carpenters, fishermen, businesswomen, and parents.

The greatest story of all will be about Jesus, born in a stable at Bethlehem. He fulfilled the Old Testament prediction. "For to us a child is born, to us a son is given ... and he will be called Wonderful Counselor, Mighty God" (Isaiah 9:6, NIV). God became flesh; the Divine was visiting mankind. Jesus grew in the normal ways that boys grow, but he was no normal boy. He lived without sin, and was the personification of pure love. He healed the sick, he forgave sins, and he did miracles such as calming a thunderstorm on Lake Galilee, as well as feeding five thousand people with two small fish and five loaves of bread. Why? To show us what God was like.

The centerpiece of history was the death of Jesus on the cross. Jesus, the sinless One, took our sins, dying to forgive us of them. You'll say with the apostle Paul, "I am crucified with Christ: nevertheless I live; yet not I, but Christ liveth in me: and the life which I now live in the flesh I live by the faith of the Son of God, who loved me, and gave himself for me" (Galatians 2:20).

The death of Jesus is the good news that our sins are forgiven and we can go to heaven when we die. The word g*ospel* means "good news." You'll read how Jesus' followers preached this gospel to the known world in the generation after Jesus' death. Because sinful people hate the message of repentance from sin, they persecuted Jesus' followers, mocking them, putting them in prison, and even murdering them.

The last book in the Bible, Revelation, tells us about the future. You'll read of persecution and tribulation, but also you'll learn of martyrs being honored as they enter the presence of God. And as you might expect, the Bible ends with descriptions of heaven and how believers will live with God forever.

Reading the Bible is a life-changing experience. Read it over and over. Enjoy your journey from Genesis to Revelation.

Sincerely yours in Christ,

Elmer L. Towns
Lynchburg, Virginia

Introduction

What is the Bible?

We call it The Holy Bible. The name comes from *ta bibla*, which means "the books" or a collection of books. The one book called The Holy Bible is actually a collection of sixty-six books that are accepted by Christians as uniquely inspired of God, and thus, it is authoritative for what Christians believe and how they act. Each of the sixty-six books has a primary thrust, such as a biography, history, letter, poem, or personal testimony.

The Old and New Testaments

The Bible is divided into two major sections, known as the Old Testament and the New Testament. While the word *testament* usually refers to a person's will, in the original language it meant "a treaty" or "covenant." Therefore, you will sometimes find written in the front of these two sections "The Old Covenant" and "The New Covenant." The Old Testament was written between the approximate dates of 1500 B.C. to 500 B.C. in the Hebrew language, except for a few selected passages in Aramaic. The theme of the Old Testament is the preparation for the coming of Jesus Christ. The New Testament was written between the approximate dates of A.D. 36 to A.D. 96 in the Greek language. Its theme is the birth of Jesus Christ, his life, his ministry, and the growth of the New Testament church.

The Old Testament. The Old Testament is usually divided into sections. They are the Pentateuch (five books), which was written by Moses; the historical books (twelve books); poetry (five books); the Major Prophets (five books); and the Minor Prophets (twelve books).

Let's start with the Pentateuch, consisting of Genesis, Exodus, Leviticus, Numbers, and Deuteronomy.

Genesis, the first book of the Bible, describes the mighty act of God in creating the world, the development of mankind into nations, and God's establishment of the nation of Israel through Abraham.

Exodus, the second book of the Bible, describes the mighty acts of God in delivering his nation, the Israelites, from Egyptian bondage. God repeatedly identifies himself, "I am the Lord thy God, which have brought thee out of the land of Egypt, out of the house of bondage. Thou shalt have no other gods before me" (Exodus 20:2-3).

The final three books of the Pentateuch are Leviticus, which tells of the establishment of a priesthood for the nation; Numbers, which describes the wandering of God's people in the wilderness on their way to the Promised Land; and Deuteronomy, a series of sermons to prepare God's people to enter the Promised Land.

The historical books begin with the Book of Joshua, which describes the capture and settlement of the Promise Land by Israel. The Book of Judges describes the twelve tribes of Israel fighting against various enemies in the land. With each attack, God raises up a judge or military leader to deliver Israel. The Book of Ruth is the story of one immigrant to Israel who chooses to serve God and marries a wealthy landowner. Through Ruth will come the Messiah, Jesus Christ. First and Second Samuel tell the story of Israel's first King Saul, and David, the greatest king of Israel. The books of First and Second Kings focus on the political development of the kingdom by David's son, Solomon, but after him the people rebel against God and they are led into captivity in Babylon. First and Second Chronicles cover the same period as Kings but focus on Israel's history from the perspective of the priest and the temple. The Book of Ezra describes God's people returning from captivity; the Book of Nehemiah describes the rebuilding of the walls of Jerusalem; and the Book of Esther tells how God cares for his people who don't return to the Promised Land but remain under Gentile rule.

The five poetry books begin with the Book of Job, which examines the problem of evil and human suffering. Psalms is the songbook or hymnal of the Jewish people. Proverbs is a collection of pithy sayings that expresses biblical principles to guide daily living. Ecclesiastes describes the emptiness of life without God; and the Song of Solomon portrays the beauty of marriage love as a symbol of divine love.

The prophets are divided into two major divisions. The Major Prophets—Isaiah, Jeremiah, Lamentations, Ezekiel, and Daniel—are called major because of their length. The prophets speak against corruption of Israel and foretell God's immediate judgment, plus God's judgment in the last days.

The Minor Prophets—called such because they are shorter—

are the last twelve books of the Old Testament. They deal with localized preaching by the prophets against the rebellion of Israel against God and the prediction of future judgement.

The New Testament. The New Testament is divided into five sections. The first section is made up of four books called the Gospels. They describe the life, teaching, death, and resurrection of Jesus Christ. *Gospel* means "good news," in other words, that there is salvation in Jesus Christ.

The second section is the Book of Acts, which is a narrative of the coming of the Holy Spirit, the beginning of the church, and the extension of the gospel from Jerusalem to the known world by the planting of churches and the evangelization of lost people.

Then, in the third section, there are thirteen letters written by Paul to the early church explaining Christian belief, attitude, and behavior. After Paul's epistles come the remaining eight letters—called general letters because they were written by other apostles or those close to the apostles.

The last section is the book of Revelation. It tells of John's prophetic visions concerning the last days, especially the second coming of Jesus Christ. The last chapters of Revelation describe heaven and what life will be like in eternity.

A History of the Bible

Because God inspired the Bible and gave it authority, it is only natural to expect God to preserve his Bible for coming generations to read. That includes you.

In the Beginning

The first person to write God's words was Adam, and his account probably included a description of the events of creation and a genealogy of the first family (see, for example, Genesis 5:1—"This is the book of the generations of Adam"). Moses included Adam's genealogy when he wrote the first five books of the Bible. He was instructed by God to write, as a permanent memorial, how God intervened for his people (Exodus 17:14). Thus, throughout the Old Testament, certain people continued to transcribe what God said to them, or how God worked through them.

The first books written were called "original autographs," but none of these have survived. We do not have any scrap, parchment, or single page of the original handwritten material. Perhaps, in the wisdom of God, he knew that if we had the original words of the Bible, we would worship the Bible rather than worshipping God himself. But before these original documents disappeared, many copies were made. In the process of copying and recopying, (the ancient way of printing), the Bible has continued until our present time.

Ezra the scribe (approximately 450 B.C.) was the first to bring all of the various Old Testament books together into one book. Instead of many different scrolls, each containing the message of the writer, Ezra compiled them into gigantic scrolls, and they were kept in giant clay pots. Thus the Old Testament was formed.

The establishment of the synagogue system helped keep the Bible intact. The synagogue came into being after Ezra (during the years between the Old and New Testaments). There was only one temple but many synagogues. The temple in Jerusalem was the sanctuary where the presence of God himself dwelt. This was the place a conscientious Jew brought animal sacrifices to God.

Synagogues were primarily houses of teaching, so copies of Scripture were kept in these locations. Wherever a community had twelve or more Jewish families, a synagogue was built. At each synagogue, Scripture was read to the people on the Sabbath by the elders of each village. The children attended school in the synagogue, where they were taught to read so they could understand God's Word. Even the king of Israel was to have his own personal copy of the Scriptures. "When he (king) sitteth upon the throne of his kingdom, that he shall write him a copy of this law in a book.... And it shall be with him, and he shall read therein all the days of his life" (Deuteronomy 17:18-19).

Perhaps Israel continued to exist as a nation—although a small nation—when many other nations disappeared from the pages of history because through Scripture it continually communicated to its children its history, tradition, values, and love of Jehovah.

Men called scribes were given the task of making copies of the Old Testament. They copied the Word of God onto the skins of animals, some of which were nothing more than coarse leather. Soot from a fireplace was mixed with olive oil to make ink. The pen was made from the tip of a feather. A scribe would suck ink into the small barrel of the quill by squeezing it, and then squeeze again to write. By the time the New Testament was written, vellum, a processed calfskin, was being used. Later people wrote on papyrus, a crude paper made from the reed plant that grew in the Nile River or other wet places.

As the Church Grew

Originally, the message of the New Testament was preached to hearers just as Jesus Christ preached to listeners. Jesus did not write any of his messages down. The apostles and other teachers circulated the message of Christianity in spoken form, passing it from generation to generation by word of mouth. Paul taught believers in the churches he founded; but when he was absent he began communicating to them in letters, telling them what to believe, what should be their attitudes, and how they should behave.

The Old Testament became the Bible of the New Testament church before the New Testament was written. Jewish people after Jesus' death continued to read the Old Testament, but they did not understand the prophecies about him found in its pages. Paul explained their spiritual blindness: "Their (Jews) minds were blinded: for until this day remaineth the same veil untaken away in the reading of the Old Testament, which veil is done away in Christ" (2 Corinthians 3:14-15). At the same time, Christians used the Old Testament to preach the New Testament gospel because they understood the prophecies. Jesus had sent them the Holy Spirit as he promised, saying "He shall teach you all things" (John 14:26).

Quite early, the church felt a need for a written account of the teachings of Jesus. The early church believed that Matthew, the tax collector who became an apostle, was the first to write a narrative of Jesus' life. This seems natural, because before Jesus called him, Matthew had recorded the taxes he collected. As he followed Jesus, he wrote down the sermons of Jesus and the events leading up to the miracles. Matthew's account was followed by those of Mark, Luke, and then John.

Because the church was growing so rapidly, many converts were unable to hear the apostles or others who had heard the original words of Jesus. They needed a written record to help them memorize the words of Jesus. Also, they wanted to read the actual words that Paul had written to the churches. Therefore, a collection of these "writings" was made for the instruction of new believers who now were a few generations removed from the apostles.

These collections happened spontaneously in the new churches springing up over the Mediterranean world. Many times Christians met in a large home of one of the believers. This was usually the home of a wealthy person who had a large dining area or courtyard where Christians could assemble. Slowly, the young churches began gathering copies of authoritative books for preaching and teaching. Most wealthy believers had a servant trained as a scribe. They would borrow copies of Paul's letters or the Gospels from other churches so their scribe could reproduce their own copy. When they couldn't borrow a copy, a scribe was sent to make copies to bring back. Within a period of four hundred years, there were hundreds of thousands of copies made. Today there are approximately fifty thousand ancient copies in part or whole for us to study or compare, representing many forms of Scripture from the early church.

Originally, the Bible was written in paragraph form much like the present-day books you read. Those leaders who followed the apostles divided the thoughts into chapter and verses, but it was not until 1228 that an English clergyman, Archbishop of Canterbury Stephen Langton, divided the books into the chapters we use today.

The Dead Sea Scrolls

The Dead Sea Scrolls discovered in 1947 are another important source of Scripture. A young shepherd boy near the Qumran community in Israel was tending his sheep in a wadi or dry riverbed. His sheep began climbing a nearby hill and he threw a dirt clod above them, expecting the dirt to splatter against the canyon wall to scare his sheep back down to the valley floor. But the dirt clod sailed into a small cavern and he heard a "clunk." He knew he had broken up a clay pot. Inside, he discovered several clay pots, each containing scrolls of the Old Testament. The boy sold them to an uncle for five dollars, who in turn sold them for fifty dollars. Today, these scrolls are invaluable. Called the Dead Sea Scrolls because they were found near the Dead Sea, they have given insight into the early forms of Scripture.

Up until the finding of the Dead Sea Scrolls, the earliest copies of Old Testament books dated back to about A.D. 1200. But the Dead Sea Scrolls date back to 200 B.C. Many thought that the Dead Sea Scrolls would reveal all types of errors that slipped into the various copies of the Bible. The opposite was true. The Bible that was copied by hand over many centuries was accurate because of scribes' commitment to preserving God's Word without alteration and the "quality control" formulas they used to guarantee the word-for-word accuracy of what they copied.

Bible Versions and Translations

Many people think that the fact that there are various translations available in bookstores today is a recent phenomenon. Not so. From the very beginning, as the apostles went out preaching the gospel to the nations of the world, they translated the

Word of God into the language of their hearers. While Hebrew and Greek were the original languages, the Bible was translated into Syrian, Coptic, Gothic, and Latin languages. Jerome's translation of the Bible in the late fourth century is known as the Latin Vulgate and became the Bible standard for over a thousand years because the clergy and laity read Latin. In time, the Word of God appeared in many other languages.

During the end of the Middle Ages, John Wycliffe translated the Bible from Latin into the language of the English people of his day. All Wycliffe's copies were handwritten. Then Johannes Gutenberg invented moveable type and the printing press was developed. The first book printed was the German Bible. Then English versions of the Bible were printed: the Cloverdale Bible, the Geneva Bible (the ones the Puritans read on the Mayflower when coming to America), and finally The King James Version (KJV) in 1611. The King James was the product of thirty-seven scholars divided into six teams who translated the entire Bible, a project authorized by the king of England. It won worldwide acceptance among the English-speaking world.

Since 1611, many other translations have appeared, including the Douay-Rheims version, translations by Moffatt and Goodspeed, the Revised Standard Bible, the Jerusalem Bible, the Amplified Bible, and the American Standard Version.

The Good News Bible appeared in 1966, issued by the American Bible Society; it was also called Today's English Version. Instead of translating the Bible word for word, it used "dynamic equivalency," which meant that the Bible was translated idea for idea so that the modern reader would understand the thinking of the original writers. A modern reader could read God's Word in his own terminology.

The New American Standard Bible (NASB) was released in 1971 after a group of scholars spent eleven years of careful scholarly work to produce the most dependable translations from the Greek and Hebrew text. Today, many careful Bible students prefer this version because it faithfully translates every word from Hebrew and Greek into English in the original sequence of words. In contrast, The New International Version (NIV) was sponsored by the New York Bible Society (now the International Bible Society), and was released in the 1970s, following the "dynamic equivalence" approach. Unlike previous translations, it referred to God as "You" instead of "Thee," "Thou," and "Thy."

The New King James Version (NKJV) appeared in the early 1980s. Thomas Nelson Publishers of Nashville, Tennessee, assembled a team of 130 Bible scholars to translate the Bible from the earliest and most trustworthy Hebrew and Greek texts, yet preserved the majestic style of the King James.

The Living Bible (LB) is a paraphrase prepared by Kenneth Taylor for his children because they had difficulty understanding the King James. It appeared first as Living Letters in 1962, which was his translation of the New Testament epistles. The entire Bible appeared in 1971, and is especially popular among young people because it expresses the Bible in contemporary language they can understand. Technically, the Living Bible is not a translation but a paraphrase. It adds words and phrases to interpret the meaning of the Bible.

At one time, those who wanted a Bible had one choice of color on the cover—black. They also had two other choices—the regular Bible, or the Red Letter Edition, which printed the words of Jesus in red. But things have changed. Now, you can get Bibles in almost every color and size. You can find Bibles specialized for couples, young people, children, or branches of the armed services. Computers provide flexibility for printing Bibles with special notes for radio speakers, organizations, small groups, and focus groups. It's not an exaggeration to say there seems to be a new translation every year, and a new reference Bible every week. As you choose a new Bible, a helpful resource is the book, *How to Choose a Bible Version,* by Robert L. Thomas.

Reference Bibles. A reference Bible has footnotes and explanations to help Bible readers interpret the Scriptures as they read. These are especially helpful for the reader who does not understand events, ideas, and words. Visit your local Christian bookseller and choose one that fits your needs.

Conclusion

The Bible is God's Book, written to give you his message. God has preserved his Word over the centuries. Today we have more Bibles and more study tools than ever before. All of these aids are prepared to help you read and understand God's message to you. God has protected his Word in the past and he always will. You can have great trust in its message, "The grass withers, the flower fades. But the Word of our God stands forever" (Isaiah 40:8, NKJV).

Chapter 1

Read the Bible With Everything You've Got

My Uncle Sam told my cousin and me stories as we sat on the front porch of his farm in South Carolina. To make sure we paid attention, he'd always say, "Listen with your eyes." I thought that was a funny expression. Everyone knows you listen with your ears, not your eyes. But Uncle Sam was a master storyteller who knew that when wiggling boys' eyes were fastened on him, they were really listening.

When you read the Bible, God wants your full attention. It's possible to have your eyes on the Bible text, but your heart and mind on another topic. I don't think it's a good practice, for instance, to read the Bible when watching television. Neither should you read your Bible between plays at a football game. Like Uncle Sam, God would tell you, listen to the Bible with your eyes and ears. In fact, you need to put everything you have into the Word. Read the Bible with all your senses—your sight, your hearing, your touch, your taste, and your smell.

1. *Read with your ears.* First, try reading out loud. When you *hear* the Bible you gain insight you'd never get by reading silently. Sometimes when you run your eyes over the passage,

your mind shifts into neutral and you don't interact with the words. It even happens to experienced Bible readers. I recently was reading Psalm 23 where it says "The Lord is my Shepherd.... He leads me beside still waters." My eyes continued onto the words of the next verses, but my mind began thinking about a green meadow and a pool of crystal water. That doesn't happen when you read aloud.

Reading out loud is hard to do when others are around. Also, most of us are not trained to read aloud. But try it when alone. You'll be amazed at how it enriches your comprehension.

You also can listen to recordings of the Bible, such as those available on cassette tapes or CD. As you listen to the passage carefully spoken, your mind won't struggle to pronounce the words but will focus on the message.

There is something even more important than the mechanics of reading with your ears. Jesus said, "Those having ears to hear..." (Matthew 11:15, 13:43), suggesting we must take full advantage of the message when we're listening to God. At another place Jesus said, "Having ears, they hear not..." (Mark 8:18), indicating some can audibly hear words, but they refuse to understand the meaning of God's message to them. So reading is important, listening is important, but understanding is the thing that counts.

When a composer sets out to compose new music, he or she must listen for the "song" within the song. It must be more than just melody, although melody is necessary to give it movement. It must be more than just rhythm, because a song doesn't have feeling without rhythm. It must have more than just chords, even though the blend of chords is the glue that holds a song together. Great music has something heard only with the heart. It is the same when reading the Bible. Look for the "song" within the song, which is the message that God speaks to your heart. Listen for the love of God behind the words on paper. In other words, *read with your ears.*

2. *Read with your mouth.* You might think I'm speaking of reading out loud. But remember God invites you to "open wide your mouth and I will fill it" (Psalm 81:10b, NIV). This is not a literal picture of God pouring something into your mouth. Just as our mouth receives air, food, and drink for physical life, so we must open our inner being to receive spiritual life. This is another way of saying open your whole heart when reading the Bible.

To read with your mouth is a picture of your inner person drinking the message of the Bible. Have you ever wanted to know God so badly that you leaped from verse to verse, devouring their message?

> As the deer pants for the water brooks, So pants my soul for You, O God. My soul thirsts for God, for the living God. When shall I come and appear before God? My tears have been my food day and night, while they continually say to me, "Where is your God?"
>
> PSALM 42:1-3, NKJV

When you're hungry, your taste buds begin to water at even the smell of hamburgers frying with a few onions sprinkled in. Your whole being gets ready for the first bite, the initial satisfaction. Bible reading should give you the same feeling. As you read the Word of God, strength and goodness fill your life. This is what Jeremiah meant when he wrote,

> Your words were found, and I ate them, And Your word was to me the joy and rejoicing of my heart; For I am called by Your name, O Lord God of hosts.
>
> JEREMIAH 15:16, NKJV

3. *Read with your nose.* That sounds funny, doesn't it? But smell is one of the senses that opens up the world around you.

Think what you'd miss if you couldn't smell. I have had sinus problems since my youth. I even took allergy shots for twenty years and had an operation to correct as much of the problem as possible. I still can't smell much. When my wife and I walked through a pineapple factory in Hawaii, she cried because the smell was so wonderful, but she was also weeping for me because I couldn't enjoy the aroma with her.

Just as you appreciate the smell of fresh picked strawberries on a spring morning, your heart figuratively melts under the refreshing aroma of the Rose of Sharon, which is a Bible picture of Jesus. Just as you smell fresh biscuits from a warm oven, you figuratively yield to the enticing aroma of Jesus, the living Bread of Life. And just as you breathe air for your physical lungs, you figuratively breathe the Bible as air to your soul.

If you read with just your eyes—and not your nose—you'll miss some of the exciting emotions of Bible reading. Obviously, you don't smell your Bible (but I do love the rich smell of a new leather-covered Bible). But allow your Bible reading to remind you of some smells as you dwell on Jesus cooking fresh fish over an open fire on the shore of Lake Galilee, or the smell of grapes and broken bread at the Lord's Supper. What do you smell when you read Psalm 23? If you close your eyes, you can smell grass and earth or the animal smell of sheep lying at the shepherd's feet. "The Lord is my shepherd; I shall not want. He makes me to lie down in green pastures; He leads me beside the still waters" (Psalm 23:1-2, NKJV).

4. *Read with your touch.* This does not suggest Braille for the blind or sign language for the deaf. Through touch you awaken your senses to understand what's around you. Sometimes the only way we know the world is through touch. For instance, plastic has replaced so many traditional things. You think you're looking at a beautiful marble stone counter in the bathroom, but it's counterfeit. While the eyes might be deceived, touch can feel the difference.

Therefore, imagine that you're touching the things you read about, and thus evoke your feelings. This should mean two things to you. First, let the feelings of the passage communicate to you. If you read about a hot day, feel the intense heat so you understand what is being communicated. At the place where Abraham met God, the temperature still soars over 100 degrees in the summer.

But don't just look for the physical feelings of the body, look to the soul. Try to determine what the people you're reading about felt. Enter into their experiences and you'll read at a deeper level.

There is a second thing about feelings. When you come to the Bible, be aware of *your* feelings as you read. Your feelings will probably determine what you get from your Bible reading. So at times, you will want to read those passages that will speak to your inner feelings.

What to read:	In time of need:
Psalms 35, 41:9-13, 55:12-23; Luke 17:3-4; Romans 12:14, 17, 19.	A FRIEND FAILED YOU
Psalms 1:1-2; 4:8, 5:8, 46, 107; Romans 5:1-5; Colossians 3:15; 2 Corinthians 4:8-10, 16-17.	NEED OF PEACE
Psalms 4, 6, 25, 42, 51; Matthew 6:5-15; Luke 1:1-14; John 17; 1 John 5:14-15.	NEED OF PRAYER
Psalms 23, 37:1-17, 55:22, 90:12-17; Philippians 4:4-7; 1 John 3:1-3.	WHEN DISCOURAGED
Matthew 26:39; 2 Timothy 2:3; Hebrews 12:1-11; James 5:11-15; 1 Peter 4:12-13, 19.	SICK OR IN PAIN
Psalms 107; Philippians 4:6; 1 Peter 5:6; Hebrews 13:5.	WHEN ANXIOUS
2 Timothy 1:7; Hebrews 4:16.	FACING CRISIS

5. *Read with your eyes.* Obviously your eyes are open when you read, and you are looking at the words on the pages. This means your eyes do more than see words on paper. "Your eyes are the window of the soul." Remember, a window works in two directions. First, you can look out, and second, outsiders can look in. So, as you are looking out at the Bible (reading it), light is entering into your heart from its pages. The world and its experiences enter your life through your eyes.

Because your eyes are a two-way channel, they can take you to a land you've never visited—to see the splendors of Jerusalem, to Egypt with Joseph in slavery, on Paul's missionary trips. Your eyes can take you to heaven, a real place where real people will spend a real eternity.

> And I saw a new heaven and a new earth, for the first heaven and the first earth had passed away. Also there was no more sea. Then I, John, saw the holy city, New Jerusalem, coming down out of heaven from God, prepared as a bride adorned for her husband.
>
> REVELATION 21:1-2, NKJV

> And he showed me a pure river of water of life, clear as crystal, proceeding from the throne of God and of the Lamb. In the middle of its street, and on either side of the river, was the tree of life, which bore twelve fruits, each [tree] yielding its fruit every month. And the leaves of the tree were for the healing of the nations.
>
> REVELATION 22:1-2, NKJV

Pick up your Bible. You are now holding God's words to you in your hands. Treat it reverently. As a boy I was taught never to put anything on a Bible, especially books or magazines. While some consider this an extreme attitude, it at least conveyed to my young mind a sense of reverence for the Bible.

The Bible is your one possession that will enable you to see into heaven. All other books that describe heaven, if what they tell you is not based on the Bible, are only guessing.

Also, the Bible is the only book that can accurately describe God. If what they tell you is not based on the Bible, all other books about God are only guessing. Like blind people groping for a door in a doorless room, they are looking for something they can't find.

But there is a God in heaven who has chosen to reveal himself to us in the Bible. All of the philosophers who search after God outside the Bible haven't found him.

We can summarize the conclusion of the ancient church leaders this way, "When I searched for God I couldn't find him, until I discovered he has been searching for me all the time. When I tried to find him, I couldn't learn about him apart from the Word of God. But while I was searching for him, he had already told me what he is like. So when I found God in the Scriptures, I came to know him and love him."

If people can't know God, what can they do? They can stand by the one-way street that comes from heaven. You can find that street in the Bible. Don't approach the Bible to project your thoughts about God onto its pages. No! Come to the Bible to discover what God says about himself and his plan for your life.

Chapter 2

Let God Tell You How to Read the Bible

Over a hundred years ago a young ministerial student asked the great evangelist D.L. Moody about what he should do after seminary. Moody knew the young man's father, so he said, "Don't go into business, your father is wealthy and you have more money than you will ever need. Devote your life to teaching the English Bible."

The young man was flustered by Moody, answering simply, "I don't know the English Bible."

The wise old evangelist Moody asked, "Don't you go to a religious college where you have professors who teach you the Bible?"

"Yes, I do have Bible classes, but I have listened to one professor lecture for six months and we still haven't determined who wrote the first five books of the Bible."

Moody told the young man, "Read the Bible on your own, read it again and again until you master its contents." The young man took his advice and became one of the great Bible teachers of his day. R.A. Torrey wrote many books and eventually became dean of the large Bible Institute of Los Angeles, now Biola University.

Just as reading the Bible changed R.A. Torrey's life, it can do the same for you. Learn to read the Bible the way God intends for you to read by following the principles for reading found in the Word of God itself. Since the Bible was inspired by God, let him tell you how to read his book.

Perhaps the best set of principles for Bible reading is found in the response of the Berean Christians to the ministry of the apostle Paul. Before coming to Berea, Paul had preached the Gospel in Thessalonica and established a young church. When he was preaching in the synagogue at Thessalonica, the Jews rejected the message of Jesus Christ. These enemies of the Gospel threatened Paul's life and ran him out of town. It was then that he fled to Berea, a small town a short distance away. As was Paul's custom, he entered the synagogue in that town to preach. The people in Berea were different; they listened to the apostle Paul and became exemplary Christians.

The following verse gives six responses of the Berean Christians that suggest principles of how to read the Bible: "These were more fair-minded than those in Thessalonica, in that they received the word with all readiness, and searched the Scriptures daily to find out whether these things were so" (Acts 17:11).

1. *Read the Bible itself.* The Christians in Berea were called "noble" because they received the Word of God preached by Paul. They were not interested in Paul's appearance, his method of preaching, his humor, or his report of current events. Even though most of them were Jews, they didn't want to examine Jewish history or what the rabbis said. Instead, they simply "received the Scriptures."

This suggests you should begin reading the Bible. Later you will want to consult what godly authorities have said about it.

Some people mistakenly think, "Oh, I would learn the Bible so much better if I had a great teacher to give me personal instructions." That is not so. God knows the Bible better than any human teacher. If you think the Bible is difficult to understand, take your problem to him and pray like David,

"Open thou mine eyes, that I may behold wondrous things out of thy law" (Psalm 119:18). You will find that God will answer and send the Holy Spirit to teach you the Bible. "When he, the Spirit of truth, is come, he will guide you into all truth" (John 16:13). Some of the humblest believers with very little formal education have become masters of the Word of God, and so gained the wisdom of God. Why is that? They prayed for the Holy Spirit to teach them the Word of God. So don't begin with a human instructor, when you can have a divine one.

Some people read their Sunday school teacher's manual before they read the Word of God. While they can get much help from a manual, always go to the Word of God first. Don't begin your study with books about the Bible. Obviously these books have their value, but begin by reading God's Word. Let the Lord speak directly to you, he can do that when you open your mind to receive the message God has for you. Be like the Berean Christians, "They received the Word."

When you pick up your Bible, find a quiet place where you can be alone with God and his Word. As you open the Bible and get ready to read, first realize that you have come into the very presence of God. When you realize God is present everywhere, and he loves you, it will revitalize the time you spend in the Word. Realize that God is going to speak to you through his Word. God is actually talking to you. When you read the Bible, you are establishing personal companionship with God each day. Think of Mary, who sat at the feet of Jesus, asking him questions and learning from him. Each day when you read the Word of God, you sit at the feet of Jesus to listen to his voice. This will make your Bible reading a wonderful journey, not just a mechanical performance of a daily duty. You are taking a trip each day into the Word of God. Your trip will take you through the Holy Land as you walk the dusty roads with Jesus. Your trip will take you into the lives of men and women who lived for God, who served him, and who worshiped him. And as you read of their victories and defeats, you take the journey with them.

2. *Read the Bible diligently.* The Berean Christians, "received the word with all readiness." When you study the Word of God, don't just casually read it as you might scan an advertisement received in the mail. Rather, read the Bible carefully; drink in every word.

Don't be in a hurry to get through your Bible reading. One of our human faults is that we want to hurry up and get through with our projects. You must take time to let God speak to you. You will only benefit from your Bible reading by applying its message to your heart. The Bible has no magic power to help you if you don't understand what it is saying. It's better to read a few verses attentively than to read a dozen chapters quickly or thoughtlessly.

When a verse "grabs" you, *stop* ... meditate ... apply. Don't hurry. Slow down and think about what God is saying to you.

As you read those things that impress you, mark them in your Bible. You don't need an elaborate marking system, simply use a pencil, pen, or highlighter to record what has impressed you, circling or underlining words or verses that you want to remember.

3. *Read the Bible "word for word."* The Bereans "searched the Scriptures," which means they looked at every word. When you read the Bible don't casually skip over words, but focus in on every word. It is God's own book and he put every word in place, therefore every word is important. Ask yourself why it is there. Get out a dictionary to look up the meaning of important words. You might decide to get a reference Bible with a center column reference to look up other verses that have the same meaning. One man went to the great Bible teacher R.A. Torrey and asked,

"Tell me in one word how to study the Bible."

"That is not easy, but if I could use only one word it would be *thoughtfully.*"

The Berean Christians examined the Scriptures because they were not satisfied to merely listen to stories or sermons. As they "searched" the Scriptures, which is the King James word, they were looking at it word for word. The word that is translated "searched" or "examined" comes from a word used of a woman in the kitchen preparing to bake bread. She *sifts* her flour so that every particle of flour is separated from another. When you *search* or *examine* the Scriptures, it is the same word for *sifting* flour to separate every particle. You're searching every word.

The Berean Christians were not satisfied to just hear what Paul said. They wanted to know if the things he was preaching were accurate. So they looked at every word that he used to make sure that there were no mistakes in his message, and that every word of his sermon agreed with every word in Scripture.

To sift the Scriptures means you must study the Bible systematically. All of your time can be fretted away by reading the Bible randomly. If you read a page or two in Genesis, and the next day read a couple of Psalms, and then you read something from the Gospels, you will not get as much out of your Bible study as you desire. (It's like the woman having flour all over her kitchen in little piles!) If you had invested the same amount of time in a systematic reading of God's Word, you would get far greater results.

A good way to begin your Bible reading is with the Gospel of John. Even though other illustrations in this book have suggested some people have begun at other places, the author recommends that a new believer begin reading the Gospel of John because it is written to convince you that Jesus is the Christ, the Son of God. If you read John carefully your belief in Jesus will be stronger and you will have further assurance of salvation and eternal life. "But these [recorded events] are written, that you may believe that Jesus is the Christ, the Son of God, and that by believing you may have life in his name" (John 20:31, NIV).

After you have read the Gospel of John through once, read it again and again until you have covered it three times. The first time through, circle the word *believe.* It occurs ninety-eight times in the King James Version. This is the theme of the Gospel of John, and it will stir belief in your heart. The second time, circle the word *life;* it occurs thirty-five times, and it helps you realize that when you believe, God will give you eternal life. The third time through, circle the word *Father.* Jesus came to tell the Jewish nation that the mighty God of Israel who had dwelt in the fearful Shekinah-Glory cloud was also their intimate and personal Father. They thought this was blasphemy, but for us it is good news.

Next, read through the Gospel of Matthew, then Mark, and finally Luke. "Gospel" means "good news," and these books bring to your heart the good news of salvation through Jesus.

Where next? Go into the book of Acts, and read it at least five times to understand the history of the Church. There are five words you may want to circle when you read the book of Acts: Witness, Holy Spirit, Holy Ghost, Prayer, and Church.

By this time you might be ready to take up a systematic approach to reading the Bible. Now it might be profitable to begin at Genesis and read through the Old Testament chapter by chapter. (See Appendix 1 for a Bible reading schedule).

In addition to a daily Bible reading schedule, my pastor recommends that you read five Psalms each day and one chapter from the book of Proverbs. Why? Because Psalms are written to make you holy, and Proverbs are written to make you wise. Also, at this suggested rate, you can read the entire books of Psalms and Proverbs in one month.

As you read the Bible, recognize that God is in back of everything that you are reading. He will keep all of the promises in the Bible. "For no matter how many promises God has made, they are 'Yes' in Christ. And so through him the 'Amen' is spoken by us to the glory of God" (2 Corinthians 1:20, NIV). God will keep his promises because, "It is impossible for God to lie..." (Hebrews 6:18, NIV).

When the Bible promises something, believe it. When your feeble mind can't comprehend it, still believe it, "in hope of eternal life, which God, who cannot lie, promised before the world began" (Titus 1:2).

Recognizing God's presence as you read the Bible will change your life. Once while I was pastoring in Dallas, Texas, I was doing some carpentry work in the back of the auditorium. Gradually I became aware that someone was in the room with me. Slowly I turned around to see a small boy standing there quietly watching me. What happened? His presence changed my actions. I found that when I went back to work, I behaved differently because I was being watched. The same will happen to you when you visualize Christ standing there by you, speaking to you, and the Bible will come alive as his presence changes your actions.

4. *Read the entire Bible.* Notice that the Berean Christians were searching the entire "Scriptures." The word *Scriptures* is used in the plural to indicate they went through all of the scrolls of the Old Testament to make sure that what Paul said was accurate.

You can't really understand God until you read his entire book. All sixty-six books in the Bible have a message, and, like a wheel with sixty-six spokes, if you take away one you weaken the whole. So read all of the Bible to understand all that God has for you.

Dr. Ashe Moore started teaching the book of Hebrews to young converts a century ago. He couldn't teach about that one book by itself. There were so many questions regarding the ceremonial law in the book of Hebrews that he began teaching the book of Leviticus as a foundation for them. His young converts asked still more questions. So eventually he decided to go back to the book of Genesis to give adequate foundation for all his Bible lectures.

If you have never read the Bible through, plan to do so now. Begin now and continue reading. There may be some things you don't understand, but don't get discouraged, keep reading. Theodore Epp, speaker on "Back to the Bible" radio broadcast, once said, "I had to read through the Bible ten times before I really got the big picture of what God was doing."

But as I have said before, don't read it too quickly. G. Campbell Morgan, a Bible teacher from England who lived a hundred years ago, said one could read through the Bible at pulpit rate in sixty hours. A banker challenged his statement, telling Dr. Morgan that it could be done more quickly.

"Well, Sir, the proof lies with you," responded the wise Morgan.

The banker returned to tell Morgan, "I read the whole Bible in forty hours."

G. Campbell Morgan stroked his white beard, laughed, and said, "I said *pulpit* rate—you can't trust a banker's rate."

Read it all. Some people study only pet books such as the Gospel of John, Romans, Daniel, or Revelation. Some study only one pet subject such as healing, dispensationalism, or the Second Coming. If you read the *whole* Bible, you will understand the *whole* plan of God for your life. Until you have read the whole Bible, you don't have God's complete picture.

Jesus believed in reading and teaching the whole Bible. On the first Easter Sunday afternoon two disciples were walking from Jerusalem to Emmaus. They were discouraged because their master had been crucified, and they had heard reports that someone had stolen the body. Then they were confused that others had seen the resurrected Christ. They did not know what to think. Then Jesus joined them, but they did not know it was Jesus. And what did Jesus do? "Beginning at Moses and all of the prophets, he expounded unto them in all of the Scriptures concerning himself" (Luke 24:27). In this short hike to Emmaus, Jesus covered the first five books of the Bible (Moses) and went through to the last seventeen books of the Bible (all the prophets). Later that same day Jesus said, "All things must be fulfilled, which were written in the law of Moses (the first five books) and in the prophets (the last seventeen books) and in the Psalms (all of the historical books) concerning me" (Luke 24:44).

5. *Read the Bible daily.* Note that the Berean Christians were searching the Scriptures "daily." You ought to have a regular time set aside each day for your Bible reading. If you say, "I'll read the Bible when I have the time," you'll find that pressures of the day will squeeze out Bible reading time. Don't say, "I'll read the Bible when I need it." When you need it most, you may be least able to read it. Therefore, follow a daily Bible reading plan; but don't limit yourself to an exact number of chapters to be read each day. Read more if you have time. Sometimes you will read less because a quota may put pressure on you for undue haste, skimming, or reading thoughtlessly. It may be better to set a *certain length of time* each day for a Bible study. Perhaps on Sundays you can give more time to cover larger passages of Scripture.

If you don't have a regular time, begin with a short time span, not a long one; so you won't get discouraged at the beginning. If you promise to read the Bible for an hour, you may not be able to keep your word. Start off with a shorter time that you know you can keep without becoming discouraged.

As you get into Bible reading, you'll find that it gets easier to set aside that time because you get so much from the Bible. When people ask me how I know so much about the Bible, I ask them how they know so much about television. We give our time to the things that are important in our lives.

The late Earl Cairns, Lord Chancellor of England, was one of the busiest men of his day. His wife said that no matter how late at night he reached home, he always got up at the same time every morning for prayer and Bible study before going off to work. His wife mentioned that even if he got home from Parliament at two o'clock in the morning, he was still up early to pray and read the Word. Lord Cairns is reported as saying, "If I had any success in life, I attribute it to the habit of giving the first two hours of each day to Bible reading and prayer."

It's important to choose the right time of day for this study. Lord Cairns chose the early morning hour because that was best for him. Some will be freshest each morning when they wake up. That's when they should read their Bible. But others are late-night people, they seem to kick it into high gear when 10:00 P.M. comes around. These people get more out of their Bible reading before they go to bed. Just do the bulk of your Bible reading when your mind is freshest and your body is strongest. Whatever time you set apart for Bible reading, keep it sacred, because you are meeting the Lord God of the Universe.

6. *Read the Bible with faith.* The Christians in Berea studied the Scriptures carefully because they wanted to "find out whether these things were so." They measured everything against the Word of God, knowing that they would find their answers in the Scriptures. Read the Bible and believe it. The apostle Paul wrote to the Christians in Thessalonica and told them, "We also thank God continually because, when you received the word of God, which you heard from us, you accepted it not as the word of men, but as it actually is, the word of God, which is at work in

you who believe" (1 Thessalonians 2:13, NIV). Will this happen in your life? Since the Bible is the Word of God, you will get the most of it out by acknowledging it for what it really is.

As you read the Bible, place your complete reliance on it. Those who read God's Word should say of any promise, no matter how challenging, that, "I will claim this for myself." Then mark the promise, claim it, and expect God to fulfill it in your life.

To grow in your faith, you must yield yourself to God, resolving to do exactly what God tells you to do. Nothing will help you understand the Bible better than your commitment to do exactly what it tells you to do. Jesus said, "If anyone chooses to do God's will, he will find out whether my teaching comes from God or whether I speak on my own" (John 7:17, NIV).

You will find that many passages that seem obscure will become clear if you are willing to obey everything that the Bible teaches. On the other hand, what happens when you start disobeying parts of the Bible? First, you will lose your thirst for the message of the Bible, and second, your mind will become blinded to the teaching of God's Word.

When you obey one truth in the Bible, you prepare yourself to see other truths in God's Word.

Chapter 3

There Are Lots of Good Reasons to Read the Bible

Harold didn't know much about Christianity or how to become a Christian. But he knew there was an emptiness in his life that only God could fill. He had examined other religions but was drawn to Christianity. He talked to a couple of friends at work who called themselves Christians, and when he asked them what he must do, they replied, "Come to church with us." Harold didn't want to go to church, he wanted to find God.

Over the next couple of years, the inner vacuum became more uncomfortable. Then he told a friend about how everyone wanted him to go to church with them. "I don't know which church is the right one. I just want to find God," he said.

His friend was wise enough to not compare one church to another. When a person is searching for God, he doesn't need to hear people criticize churches or even compare churches. What he needs is to hear from God.

"All churches claim to believe in the Bible, so read the Bible for yourself to find out what it says about God," Harold's friend said. "When you find out what the Bible says about God, then go to the church that comes closest to the Word of God."

The friend gave Harold a Bible and told him to start by reading the Gospel of John. There he would learn about Jesus Christ, the center of Christianity. "You will find God by learning about Jesus Christ," the friend said.

Harold began reading the Gospel of John, staying up late to devour the Scriptures. Like a hungry man, he couldn't get enough. After reading John two or three times, Harold shut the door to his room and knelt. "Lord Jesus, I believe in you," Harold said simply.

Harold had understood the message of John. It is a book that tells people to believe in Jesus Christ to have eternal life (remember, the word *believe* occurs in the King James version ninety-eight times). Harold was converted by reading the Bible. But that is only one of the reasons why you read the Bible; we'll look at some of the many others.

> But these are written that you may believe that Jesus is the Christ, the Son of God, and that by believing you may have life in his name.
>
> JOHN 20:31, NIV

1. *You will find eternal life by reading the Bible.* When Jesus preached a "hard" sermon to the multitude at the synagogue in Capernaum, many people murmured about the sermon. Jesus told them, "The words that I speak unto you, they are spirit, and they are life" (John 6:63). This means that the Bible has the words of God that give eternal life, but the multitudes didn't like his sermon, so they left. Then Jesus asked his disciples if they were planning to leave also. Peter answered, "Lord, to whom shall we go? Thou hast the words of eternal life" (John 6:68).

Peter understood what Jesus had preached—the message of eternal life. The Bible has it. You must read God's Word to get that message.

One companion of the apostle Paul on his missionary journeys was Timothy, a young man Paul led to salvation when he first visited Asia Minor, the region we know today as Turkey. When Paul wrote to Timothy, he highlighted the role that the Bible had in preparing him for salvation. It was the Word of God that planted the seed of faith in Timothy's heart, and that seed grew to full salvation. Therefore, read the Word of God to find eternal salvation in Jesus Christ.

> I call to remembrance the unfeigned faith that is in you, (Timothy) which dwelt first in your grandmother Lois and your mother Eunice, and I am persuaded is in you also.... But you continue in the things which you have learned and been assured of, knowing from whom you have learned them, and that from childhood you have known the Holy Scriptures, which are able to make you wise for salvation through faith which is in Christ Jesus.
>
> 2 TIMOTHY 1:5; 3:14-15, NKJV

2. *You will be protected from sin by reading the Word of God.* Christians should be living victorious lives, overcoming their bad habits and the sins that trip them up. (A sin is simply disobeying God). But some Christians are continually falling into old sins or find new temptations. Even the apostle Paul knew the battle: "For I know that in me (that is, in my flesh,) dwelleth no good thing: for to will is present with me; but *how* to perform that which is good I find not" (Romans 7:18). In contrast,

David learned the secret to overcoming when he wrote, "Thy word have I hid in mine heart, that I might not sin against thee" (Psalm 119:11).

A pastor gave a Bible to a young man who kept falling into sin. "This Bible will keep you from sin—or sin will keep you from the Bible," he said.

How does the Bible give us victory? First of all, the Bible has instructional power, teaching you the correct way to live for God. "Thy word is lamp unto my feet, and a light unto my path" (Psalm 119:105). Historian Arnold Toynbee said, "It (the Bible) pierces through the intellect and preys directly upon the heart."

There is another way the Bible will keep you pure. It will cleanse your conscience, eradicate your guilt, and purify your soul. Jesus said, "Now ye are clean through the Word which I have spoken to you" (John 15:3).

In a third way, the Bible will correct any wrong teaching that allows for deviant behavior. Paul reminded Timothy that the Word of God would correct false ideas. "All Scripture is given by inspiration of God, and is profitable for doctrine, for reproof, for correction, for instruction in righteousness." (2 Timothy 3:16, NKJV)

Also, the Bible will protect from sin by building a "hedge" of protection against sin.

> But be doers of the word, and not hearers only, deceiving yourselves. For if anyone is a hearer of the word and not a doer, he is like a man observing his natural face in a mirror; for he observes himself, goes away, and immediately forgets what kind of man he was. But he who looks into

> the perfect law of liberty and continues in it, and is not a forgetful hearer but a doer of the work, this one will be blessed in what he does.
>
> JAMES 1:22-25, NKJV

3. *You grow in faith by reading the Word of God.* The Bible describes receiving Jesus Christ as being born into God's family. "Yet to all who received him, to those who believed in his name, he gave the right to become children of God" (John 1:12, NIV). Five times in the Scriptures Christians are described as babies or children who need to grow through the Word of God. (See 1 Corinthians 3:1-3; 4:14-21; Hebrews 5:11-14). Perhaps the best known of these verses is 1 Peter 2:2 (NIV)—"Like newborn babies, crave pure spiritual milk, so that by it you may grow up in your salvation." You grow as a Christian as you read the Word of God. Just as milk makes babies strong, so the Scriptures make you strong in the faith.

A man of God once told me that every reference in the Bible to growing was connected to knowing and obeying the Word of God. I think he was right. You must read the Bible so you can know and obey God's Word. Remember, the Bible is milk for the body (1 Peter 2:2), meat for the growing Christian (Hebrews 5:12-14), bread for the hungry (John 6:51), and honey for satisfaction (Psalm 19:10).

What happens to your body when you don't eat properly? You begin to feel weak, and eventually you get sick. The longer you stay away from food, the weaker and sicker you become. The same with the Word of God. If you don't read the Word of God on a regular basis, you will become a weak Christian and eventually a sickly Christian. Therefore, "Grow in grace, and in the knowledge of our Lord and Savior Jesus Christ" (2 Peter 3:18).

> The statutes of the Lord are right, rejoicing the heart: the commandment of the Lord is pure, enlightening the eyes. The fear of the Lord is clean, enduring for ever: the judgments of the Lord are true and righteous altogether.
>
> PSALM 19:8-9

4. *You will hear the words of God by reading the Bible.* If your heart is troubled, you can hear God speaking peace to you when you read the Bible. It is the same with depression or loneliness. When you read the Word of God, you can hear the Lord and he will meet the needs of your heart. For many years now, The Gideons International organization has placed Bibles in hotel and motel rooms. The organization's files are filled with stories of individuals who have contemplated suicide, divorce, or acts of violence. But when troubled people have picked up the Bible and followed the Gideon guide, "When In Trouble," they have read the Word of God and it has changed their lives.

You can hear God speak to you by his Spirit when you read the words of Scripture. I heard the founding president of the Republic of China, Chaing Kai-shek, testify, "The Bible is the voice of the Holy Spirit to me."

My sister Martha received Jesus Christ because she was memorizing the Word of God. Before salvation, Martha was a religious girl, never involved with any outward sin. Yet, after I became converted, I was not sure Martha had been born again. She was a church member, but not a Christian. I typed a hundred Bible verses on 3x5 cards and promised to purchase a new reference Bible for her if she could perfectly repeat all one hundred verses. As Martha quoted each verse, I helped her see what they meant, praying for God to speak to her by the Holy Spirit. Halfway through the project, she went away to camp. Phoning me long-distance, Martha told me that she came under conviction when a camp speaker began quoting verse after verse that she had memorized. She said, "Elmer, God spoke to me through those verses." She prayed to receive Christ as Savior. I am glad that God spoke to her through the Scriptures.

Two men went to a Billy Graham evangelistic crusade in England. Before the service, they struck up a conversation. Both were critical of the evangelist's methods. That night, Billy Graham kept saying over and over, "The Bible says...." When the gospel invitation was given, one man said to the other, "I don't know about you, but I am going forward to get saved." Billy Graham had only one method: it was to preach the Bible, and its message would reach people's hearts. The other man hesitated for a moment and then reached into his coat and said, "Here's your wallet that I stole. I'll go with you."

> How sweet are thy words unto my taste! Yea, sweeter than honey to my mouth! Through thy precepts I get understanding: therefore I hate every false way. Thy word is a lamp unto my feet, and a light unto my path. I have sworn, and I will perform it, that I will keep thy righteous judgments.
>
> PSALM 119:103-106

5. *You will become successful through reading the Word of God.* The Bible can turn around defeated lives, helping people live

successfully on this earth. God challenged Joshua with the following promise as he took over the leadership of Israel after Moses' death, "Do not let this Book of the Law depart from your mouth; meditate on it day and night, so that you may be careful to do everything written in it. Then you will be prosperous and successful" (Joshua 1:8, NIV). Notice three things about this verse. First of all, Joshua had to do more than just read the Scriptures; he had to memorize it and then meditate on it. In your reading of the Word of God, never just read without understanding the message. Think about what you are reading, and meditate on the Bible. A second thing God told Joshua was to make a commitment to obey the Word of God. When a person obeys God, a third thing happens, "Then thou shalt have good success." The person who knows and lives by the Word of God can be successful in his sight and in the sight of God.

The Bible is a guidebook that contains both the positive and negative principles of life. When you read and make a commitment to the Bible, you will be able to live within the framework of God's principles, which leads to success.

Some habits will disappear immediately after conversion; others will linger. In front of my window are two trees that react differently to the winter winds. The first is a locust tree that loses its leaves when the first fall wind blows; I can see the Blue Ridge Mountains through its barren limbs. Next to it is a pin oak tree whose leaves turn brown and eventually die; they do not drop off. I have watched howling winds whistle through the pin oak tree, but the leaves stick until springtime. When new life begins surging through the pin oak tree, new sap pushes off the dead leaves as new leaves appear. Some people lose their old habits immediately at conversion, like the locust tree whose leaves drop off immediately. Other people don't get rid of their past habits until they get into the Word of God and the new life of Christ push their old habits out of their life.

> Blessed [is] the man who walks not in the counsel of the ungodly, nor stands in the path of sinners, nor sits in the seat of the scornful; But his delight [is] in the law of the Lord, And in His law he meditates day and night. He shall be like a tree planted by the rivers of water, that brings forth its fruit in its season, whose leaf also shall not wither; and whatever he does shall prosper.
>
> PSALM 1:1-3, NKJV

6. *You will find solutions to your problems while reading the Bible.* The Bible is like a toolbox in the experienced mechanic's hand. When the old jalopy spits, sputters, and spews, the mechanic unconsciously reaches for the right tool in his toolbox. In the same way, when you are faced with problems in your life, you should unconsciously reach into the Bible—your spiritual toolbox—to come up with the right answer to solve your problems. Because a knowledge of the Bible is useful, it works in your life; you should read the Word of God to apply its truth to your life. So, even when you don't have time to search for the answers, you'll know what's there because you have been reading God's Word.

But more than solving problems, the Bible will keep you from getting into some problems. When you buy a new car, you get an owner's manual that tells you how to safely operate and maintain your car. I bought a new automobile in 1997, but couldn't find the trunk latch anywhere. I searched in vain, almost standing on my head on the floorboard of the car looking for the trunk latch. When I called the 800 number for help, the young voice at the other end of the phone said, "Page 86 of the owner's manual tells you where to locate your truck latch." The voice paused before explaining, "It's underneath the left armrest of the driver's seat." I felt foolish for not going to the owner's manual first. Trouble in this life is inevitable. "Man is born into trouble, as the sparks fly upward" (Job 5:7, NKJV). People need to read the Word of God to find God's solution for problems.

> You have given us your laws to obey—oh, how I want to follow them consistently. Then I will not be disgraced, for I will have a clean record. After you have corrected me I will thank you by living as I should.... Oh, don't forsake me and let me slip back into sin again.
>
> PSALM 119:4-8, LB

7. *You will find joy from reading the Bible.* What happens when you read and obey the Bible? Page after page of the Bible will tell a child of God how to live for God. As you continue reading the Bible, you find confidence and joy. Why? Because you will discover through the Scriptures, all of the riches that Christ has given to his children. Obviously, this does not mean financial riches, but knowing God intimately is the greatest treasure in life.

> Praise be to the God and Father of our Lord Jesus Christ, who has blessed us in the heavenly realms with every spiritual blessing in Christ. For he chose us in him before the creation of the world to be holy and blameless in his sight. In love he predestined us to be adopted as his sons through Jesus Christ, in accordance with his pleasure and will—to the praise of his glorious grace, which he has freely given us in the One he loves.
>
> EPHESIANS 1:3-6, NIV

These are only a few of the reasons to read the Bible. The list could include growing your character and values, breaking harmful addictions, becoming a better parent or child, becoming wise, becoming happier, or getting help in serving God. There are these and many more, so begin today.

CHAPTER 4

GETTING READY TO READ THE BIBLE

Once, when I was a young minister, I visited an elderly lady who had been criticized by another pastor because of her lack of faith. She asked me, "How can I have more faith?" At first the question scared me because it was a serious question and I didn't know much doctrine. Then I remembered a verse I had memorized that answered her question. I quoted the verse, "So then faith comes by hearing, and hearing by the word of God" (Romans 10:17, NKJV).

I told the lady she would have more faith when the Bible controlled her thinking, her loving, her decisions, her entire life. I held up my hand to the lady, explaining that each finger was necessary to grasp the Bible, and each finger represented one way to hang on to the Bible.

1. Hearing the Word of God

2. Reading Every Day

3. Studying the Bible

4. Memorizing Bible Passages

5. Meditatating on the Bible

1. The first finger is hearing the Word of God. I told the lady she would grow in faith as she attended church services to hear the preaching and reading of the Word of God. Bible classes, Sunday school, or home fellowship groups are other places where the believer can hear the Bible taught. As you listen to the Bible being read, or you read it out loud, you are fulfilling a biblical command for the Lord's blessing, "Blessed is he who reads and those who hear the words of this prophecy" (Revelation 1:3, NKJV). Make use of recorded portions of Scripture, listening to the Bible during your quiet time with God each morning. Also you can listen to the Scripture on cassette or CD as you drive. Hearing the Bible will remind you what God can do for you.

2. The second finger represents reading every day some portions of the Bible, eventually reading all the Bible at a rate that is meaningful to you. Because reading the Bible is important, Paul told Timothy, "Till I come, give attention to reading..." (1 Timothy 4:13, NKJV).

Sometimes you will want to read the short one-chapter books of the Bible. They can be covered in a brief period of time and you will get a concentrated theme from each book.

Here are some suggestions for some short books. In the Old Testament, Obadiah deals with the judgment of God's enemy. Haggai, which has two chapters, considers what God commands. In the New Testament, Philemon talks about forgiving others, since God has forgiven us. Second John is about truth in love, and Third John is about love in truth. And lastly, Jude talks about contending for the faith.

There are other passages you can read in a short period of

time. Try reading those psalms in the Book of Psalms credited to Asaph. Asaph was one of the priests who fled with David when Saul pursued him. His psalms emphasize how God protects his servants when they go through danger. Asaph remembers the "close calls" and praises God for deliverance. Asaph said "I will remember the works of the Lord; Surely I will remember Your wonders of old. I will also meditate on all Your work, And talk of Your deeds" (Psalms 77:11, NKJV). These psalms will be especially meaningful when you have trouble or difficulties.

After David was put on the throne of Israel, Asaph lived in the presence of God, and supervised the priests of God in the temple. He had oversight of singers, musicians, and the priests who served God in the tabernacle. As Asaph lay upon his bed, he remembered the cold, lonely days in the open fields, separated from family, home, and the tabernacle of God. Asaph wrote,

> I remember, in times of trouble, my songs in the night,
> I prayed constantly to the Lord,
> Will you cast me away forever,
> Is your mercy gone forever?
> I remember in infirmity, God's right hand protected me,
> I remembered His past wonders,
> I meditated all night on His works.
>
> PSALM 77 (Author's translation)

There is another section of the Book of Psalms you may want to read—those twelve written by the sons of Korah. The authorship is attributed to the sons of Korah in general, rather than a specific person. There's an intriguing reason why they didn't put a name on their psalms. Originally, Korah was the family leader, in the line of Levi (see Exodus 6:24). That meant Korah was a priest who sacrificed to God. But Moses and Aaron, also Levites, became leaders of God's people, not Korah. He became jealous. Korah, with two companions, resisted the leadership of Moses (see Numbers 16, 26:9-11, 27:3, Jude 11). Because Korah refused to appear before God as commanded, Korah, Datham, and Abirom and their followers were swallowed up by the earth in an earthquake. The children of Korah were spared (see Numbers 26:11). The sons of Korah were ashamed of their father's rebellion. Out of repentance, they followed a meek and selfless lifestyle. Never again does a son of Korah become a prideful leader, but in humility they remain in the presence of God without recognition or fanfare. Out of humility, they didn't put their individual name on their work, but ascribed their writings to the sons of Korah.

The theme of the sons of Korah is knowing God intimately. They wanted to know God and dwell in his presence in his sanctuary. A recurring theme in their psalms is the altar of God, perhaps because they remember the sin of their family namesake. When Korah wouldn't come to the sanctuary, his sons stayed close to the altar for cleansing and purity. Maybe at the altar they were kept from temptation.

The first set of the psalms of the Sons of Korah could be entitled Longing for God (42); Hoping in God (43); A Prayer for the Distressed (44); The Beauty of the King (45); Our Refuge and Strength in God (46); Celebrating the Lord God Most High (47); The Beauty of the City of Zion (48); and Discerning Real Value in Life (49). The remaining might be called Enjoying the House of God (84); The Prayer of the

Returned Exiles (85); Zion, the City of God (87); and A Lament over Affliction (88).

How amiable is your Temple, O Lord God of Hosts,
My soul longs for your courts,
My heart cries out for the Living God.
Yes, the sparrow must find a house for its young,
My home is with my God,
Even with your altar my God.
Blessed are all who desire to dwell in Your house,
They go from strength to strength.
Every one to appear before God.
I'd rather be in your court one day, than any other place one thousand,
I'd rather be a doorkeeper in God's house,
Than be rich in the tents of wickedness.
God protect me, be my sun and shield,
Lord give me grace and glory,
Don't keep any good thing from me.

PSALM 84 (Author's Translation)

There are other portions of Scripture for concentrated reading. Watch for the following themes as you read the following books. They are suggested because they are not long books. You might want to write the theme word or phrase in your Bible near the beginning of the book.

THEME	BIBLE BOOK
Victory	Joshua
In the Heavenlies	Ephesians
Grace over legalism	Galatians
Joy	Philippians
Jesus is pre-eminent	Colossians
Redemption	Ruth
Assurance	1 John

You will want to read several chapters in the Bible that have a single dominant theme. Watch for the key word in each of the following chapters. By highlighting the key word, it will make the theme more apparent.

THEME	BIBLE PASSAGE
Faith	Hebrews 11
Rest	Hebrews 4
Fasting	Isaiah 58
Love	1 Corinthians 13
Resurrection	1 Corinthians 15
Testings	James 1
Persecution	1 Peter 4

There are several things I do when reading the Bible that help me get more from my reading. If you are comfortable with any of these suggestions, try them.

Read a passage from more than one version of the Bible. I usually begin with the old standard, the King James Version. It is rich in terminology and expression. Even though a few of its words are seldom used by our modern society, because of their expressiveness, I begin here. Then I go to a couple of the modern versions, but inevitably I end up reading the Living Bible (not a Bible translation, but one man's paraphrase). Why? Just as the King James Version is rich in historic expressions, the Living Bible is rich in contemporary expression.

Next read with a good dictionary close by. (Use the *Oxford Dictionary* if you're from a former British Commonwealth country because on a few occasions they have different spellings, such as Saviour instead of Savior.)

I read with a pencil in hand to mark my Bible. Some people disagree with marking a Bible because they say the Bible must be revered. I don't feel irreverent by underlining words to emphasize meaning or by writing notes in the margins to help me remember the meaning of a passage. What's important? To me, "It's not the marks in your Bible, but the marks your Bible makes on you."

3. *Studying the Bible.* The third finger to grasp the Bible is study. Paul told Timothy, "Study to shew thyself approved unto God, a workman that needeth not to be ashamed, rightly dividing the word of truth " (2 Timothy 2:15). The original King James is quoted because the word "study" is used, suggesting you must do more than read—you must study. Modern versions use terms like "give attention" and "strive diligently," suggesting how to study. Just reading the Bible over and over is not Bible study. When you study the Bible, you dig deep below the surface.

First, find the meaning of words in the passage—not every word—but the significant words. Look in a good dictionary to find the contemporary meaning, then look in a Bible dictionary to determine how a word was used when the Bible was written. (See Appendix 1.)

Next, use a concordance to find other verses that mean the same thing. (See Appendix 1.) A concordance lists all the Scripture mentioning a certain word or phrase. Compare one verse in the Bible with other verses that have similar words or meaning. This will give you some background on the passage you are studying. If you don't have a large concordance, use the limited concordance often included in the back of a Bible. If your version has center column references, use them.

Four Steps in Bible Study

There are some things that will help you get more out of Bible study. When you study, *read with purpose.* There is little benefit in just aimlessly reading the Bible without understanding the message, or getting anything out of it. Use the following four questions to guide your thinking.

First, ask yourself *what does this passage say?* I want to amplify Rudyard Kipling's advice, "Who, how, why, where and when, these are my serving men."

Meaning is the second thing to look for in reading the Bible. Ask yourself a second question: *What does the passage mean?* Usually the answer is to look into the author's mind. What the writer meant to say, is what the Bible passage means. Don't try to "read" something into the Bible that's not there. Over 150 years ago David Cooper penned a rule to help us interpret the Bible. "When the plain sense of Scripture makes common sense, seek no other sense; therefore, take every word at its primary, literal meaning."

Next, apply the Bible to your life. Ask a third question: *How does the passage apply to me?* When you read the Bible, there is one interpretation (meaning), but many applications (how to live).

Let your fourth question focus on *problems.* If there's anything you don't understand, write it out into a question. The discipline of writing out questions often will help you find the answers. A question that's well defined is half solved.

But you need to write out more than things you don't understand. Think about the problems that the Bible solves. Write out the questions or problems that others might have that come up as you're studying the Bible. Looking at a Bible passage through the eyes of others that have questions will help sharpen your mind to be more analytical. In the long run, this will help you go deeper in the Word.

The final step in studying is writing out *practical applications* for your daily life. When you first read the passage, were you looking for ways to apply the Scripture to your life? Now write down as many practical principles as come to your mind.

4. *Memorize Bible Passages.* The fourth finger to grasp the Bible is memorizing the Bible. Whether you're very young or very old, the discipline of committing the Bible to memory will help you grow in spirituality.

First, it's important to know what verses to memorize. Don't just choose a popular verse, or one that's in your Bible reading. Choose a verse that becomes meaningful as you read it. Sometimes people say, "The verse jumped off the page." That's their way of saying a verse caught their attention or met an immediate need in their life. Choose a verse to memorize that's meaningful at the time.

Once you've got a verse in mind, mark it in your Bible so it "stands out" in the text. Then read the context to understand the background and meaning of the text. When you know the context, it will be easier to memorize.

As you repeatedly read the verse, emphasize the different

words and their place in the text. Since God put every word in the Bible for a reason, ask yourself why he put them there.

5. *Meditate on the Bible.* The fifth finger to grasp the Bible is meditation. The Bible tells you to meditate for your spiritual growth. The Book of Psalms begins with an exhortation to meditate on its context, promising that the person who repeatedly thinks about Scripture will be blessed.

> Blessed is the man who walks not in the counsel of the ungodly, nor stands in the path of sinners, nor sits in the seat of the scornful; but his delight is in the law of the Lord, and in His law he meditates day and night.
>
> PSALM 1:1-2, NKJV

Remember, God promised success to Joshua when he meditated on Scripture. You, too, can have success by constantly thinking on the Word of God.

If you find it hard to spend extended time in prayer, between times of intercession, meditate on God and his Word. Read some passages of Scripture, then come back to prayer at a later time.

Use "downtimes" to meditate on God's Word, such as when you are driving the expressway or waiting for a message to download on your computer. Use verses you are memorizing to help your meditation. Go from the task of memorizing a verse, to thinking about its meaning, to applying it to your life. Understanding the Bible is absolutely imperative to a believer's growth, and without the Bible, you can't grow in Christ, nor become like him.

Chapter 5

Reading About People in the Bible

One of the greatest pleasures you'll get from the Bible is reading its stories about people. There are over 3,500 individual people identified in the Bible. Most just have their names mentioned once, but they're each interesting in their own way. Most importantly, though, you will learn about yourself as you read about these fellow humans. Here are a few individuals to start your thinking:

- A bashful woman who was healed by Jesus (see Mark 5:25-34).
- A little boy who gave Jesus his fish and bread (see John 6:5-14).
- A man who kept giving in to temptation (see Judges 16:4-21).
- A woman immigrant who married a wealthy man (see the Book of Ruth).
- A nephew who saved the life of his famous uncle (see Acts 23:12-24).

When you read and understand the people of the Bible, you will find a wonderful world of knowledge opening up to you. Why? Because the Bible is primarily written about people from the past for God's people today. So as you read about these people, you will learn how God can speak to you and how God tries to relate to you. Do you want to learn more about God?

One of the most popular magazines on today's newsstands is *People*. Why? Because people are drawn to people. People want to find out about people. If this is true about you, focus on the people you read about in the Bible. The psalmist said, "I have rejoiced in the way of Your testimonies as much as in all riches" (Psalm 119:14, NKJV). This verse means the psalmist liked to hear the testimonies of others who walked with God.

Real People

You have a *life message*; I have a *life message*. Everyone makes a statement with his or her life, and that is the message we send to others. It may be good or bad, effective or ineffective. When you come to read about the people of the Bible, watch for their *life message*. Almost immediately when you read about Peter, you see a man who is on a spiritual cloud one day and who tumbles the next. At one point Peter denies Jesus to a little girl, and then later he speaks boldly to multitudes on the day of Pentecost. Why is he like that? You'll have to read the Bible to find out.

As you read the Bible you will notice that some personalities are major actors on the stage of Scripture. These people like Abraham, Jacob, Moses, and Mary the mother of Jesus have a major *life message* for us. But there are many minor actors on the stage of Scriptures. These are like character actors. Their story is briefly told, but even these people have a *life message* that can help enrich our lives. As an example, Enoch is

mentioned in only a few verses but he challenges us to
mately with God.

> And Enoch lived sixty and five years, and begat Methuselah: And Enoch walked with God after he begat Methuselah three hundred years, and begat sons and daughters: And all the days of Enoch were three hundred sixty and five years: And Enoch walked with God: and he was not; for God took him.
>
> GENESIS 5:21-24

As you are reading the Bible, you may want to pause and study a Bible character more exhaustively. How can you do this? First, find and read every verse in the Bible on the person. You do this by looking up his or her name in an exhaustive concordance. This may take a long time, but it may prove to be extremely profitable.

Second, if your Bible has a center column of references, trace your subject that way. They may explain other places, topics, or events about the person. By careful examination, you may find out something about the character, even when the name is not mentioned in these references.

Third, look in a Bible dictionary or encyclopedia. These will give you background, analysis, and related facts. Remember, these books are the research of a human author, so every article you read may be limited, biased, or sketchy. To assure a more balanced picture, read more than one article.

Fourth, as you study your character, look to the background. This may give you insight about motives, values, or perspective on life. Ask yourself the following questions:

- Are the person's parents or grandparents identified?
- How did the parents or grandparents influence the character of the person?
- What is the person's ethnic background?
- What are the characteristics of the times in which the person lived?

Another way to learn about people is to study their names. Antisthenes, the founder of the ancient Greek school of Cynicism, said, "The beginning of all instruction is the study of names." Your character may have more than one name. For instance, Abram ("High Father") had his name changed to Abraham ("Father of Many Nations") after he believed God. Jacob ("Deceiver") had his name changed to Israel ("Prince with God") after he wrestled all night with God. Simon's name ("listening") was changed to Peter ("Rock") when Jesus called him.

Again, you may have to go to your center cross-reference notes or dictionary to find out the meaning to their names. Sometimes children were given names because of an occupation that the parents expected them to have. At other times, a name identified the child's personality, the times, or other meanings. Note how some people lived up to their names while others disappointed their parents.

As you read about people, watch for turning points in their lives. Sometimes these can be traumatic or sensational events, such as Ruth making a decision to leave Moab, her country, and people (Ruth 1:8, 16-18). When she turned her back on Moab's idols to become an immigrant in Bethlehem and a follower of Jehovah, God rewarded her when she met and married her husband.

There are other events that are smaller and less significant, but even these can turn about the life of the person. Consider a small boy who donated his lunch of two small fish and five dinner rolls to Jesus. While it may appear insignificant, it probably changed the life of that young boy forever. Ask yourself the following questions:

- Was the future course of events affected by the birth of the person or the death of someone near the person?
- What would have happened to you if you had to live through the same circumstances?
- What were the unique encounters with God that changed the person's life? For instance, when Jacob wrestled with God all night, his name was changed to Israel.

Try to determine something of the person's character. Watch for evidence of his or her motivation. Usually a person is moved to action by his or her inner strength, or lack of it. What sort of relationships are there? That tells you how other people are valued.

As you study you'll begin to see biblical principles. The following questions will help you apply lessons to your life from the life of the Bible character you are studying.

- What were the conditions of the person's life and how did he or she respond to them?
- Did the person's name suggest any character traits that influenced his or her life? Did the person reflect or deny the meaning of the name?
- What do you know about the person from the friends with which he or she associated?

- What influence did the person have on those around him or her?
- Can you see any growth or development in the person's character as you read the story?

As you read about people in the Bible, always look at their relationship with God, asking yourself, "What can I learn about my relationship with God?" In some cases, the person might reveal the qualities of God in their life. So you might ask, "How can I become more like God?" But if a person is rebelling against the Lord, you are able to find something about God's judgment from their actions by asking, "What can I learn to avoid?"

> Then Job replied to the Lord: "I know that you can do all things; no plan of yours can be thwarted. You asked, 'Who is this that obscures my counsel without knowledge?' Surely I spoke of things I did not understand, things too wonderful for me to know.... My ears had heard of you but now my eyes have seen you. Therefore I despise myself and repent in dust and ashes...." After Job had prayed for his friends, the Lord made him prosperous again and gave him twice as much as he had before.
>
> JOB 42:1-3; 5-6, 10, NIV

Discover the Life Message

After you have completed all your reading about the person in the Bible, come back to identify the single most important thing about that person's life. What is his or her *life message*? Write it down in one or two sentences.

Most people are remembered for one event or one act of kindness. A woman interrupted a feast that Jesus attended to honor the Lord. Her act will always be remembered.

> A woman came to him with an alabaster jar of very expensive perfume, which she poured on his head as he was reclining at the table. When the disciples saw this, they were indignant.... Jesus said to them, "Why are you bothering this woman? She has done a beautiful thing to me. The poor you will always have with you, but you will not always have me. When she poured this perfume on my body, she did it to prepare me for burial. I tell you the truth, wherever this gospel is preached throughout the world, what she has done will also be told, in memory of her."
>
> MATTHEW 26:7-8, 10-13, NIV

Every person has a purpose, and when we find that purpose, we understand better why God put the person on this earth. Use the following questions to help you understand the *life message* of each person.

- How can the person's *life message* help me walk with God?
- How can the person's *life message* help me meet the challenges of my life?
- What principles of living challenge me most from the person's *life message*?
- What changes do I need to make in my life after understanding the person's *life message*?

Reading about people will serve as a background for everything you get from the Bible. The Bible is written for people and it was written about people. Therefore, read it in the same way. Read about people like yourself, read to apply the lessons learned by the people of the Bible to yourself, and grow with the people in the Bible as you grow yourself.

Chapter 6

Reading Stories in the Bible

One of Jesus' favorite methods of teaching was telling stories. Most great teachers have followed his example, because a story is one of the best ways to communicate a message. Jesus used a form of story called a parable. The Greek word *parabole* is a compound of other words; first the preposition, *para*, meaning "besides," and then the verb, *pallein*, meaning "to place or throw down." Literally, a parable means *to place one thing beside another*. Jesus was placing a story beside the application so people could see the point. A parable is an earthly story with a heavenly meaning.

Some have tried to define the word parable, calling it "an outward symbol of an inward reality." But that describes a lot of things. Just remember that a parable is an earthly story with a heavenly meaning.

You've been reading stories all your life, so why do you need help in reading parables? The answer is very simple: because parables have a point or application. You will get more out of Bible reading if you learn how to apply the meaning of parables to your life.

When a lawyer asked Jesus "Who is my neighbor?" Jesus told him of a story of a man who was robbed and beaten and left to die. Three people came by and saw the man in his desperate condition. In conclusion, Jesus answered the question "Who is my neighbor?" by applying the parable to his listeners.

The Parable of the Good Samaritan

> Jesus said, "A man was going down from Jerusalem to Jericho, when he fell into the hands of robbers. They stripped him of his clothes, beat him and went away, leaving him half dead. A priest happened to be going down the same road, and when he saw the man, he passed by on the other side. So too, a Levite, when he came to the place and saw him, passed by on the other side. But a Samaritan, as he traveled, came where the man was; and when he saw him, he took pity on him. He went to him and bandaged his wounds, pouring on oil and wine. Then he put the man on his own donkey, took him to an inn and took care of him. The next day he took out two silver coins and gave them to the innkeeper. 'Look after him,' he said, 'and when I return, I will reimburse you for any extra expense you may have.' Which of the these three do you think was a neighbor to the man who fell into the hands of the robbers?"
>
> LUKE 10:30-36, NIV

Jesus also told parables to motivate his listeners to learn what he was teaching. On one occasion Peter said, "Explain the parable to us" (Matthew 15:15, NIV). Apparently, Peter was speaking for the multitude as well as himself; they all needed more instruction.

In the third place, Jesus used parables to apply the lessons directly to the hearers' lives. He said to his disciples,

> Now learn this parable from the fig tree: When its branch has already become tender and puts forth leaves, you know that summer is near. So you also, when you see all these things, know that it is near, even at the door! Assuredly, I say to you, this generation will by no means pass away till all these things are fulfilled. Heaven and earth will pass away, but My words will by no means pass away. But of that day and hour no one knows, no, not even the angels of heaven, but My Father only.
>
> MATTHEW 24:32-36, NKJV

Finally, Jesus gave parables to challenge his listeners. When he finished telling the story of the Good Samaritan, Jesus commanded, "Go and do likewise" (Luke 10:37, NKJV).

A parable is a story that is true to life, but parables are not retelling stories of actual events that occurred. Jesus made these stories up to apply his lessons to the contemporary life of his listeners. However, he did not use mythical creatures as the Greeks did with their flying horses or centaurs nor talking animals like those of American fairytales.

That's not to say Jesus' parables weren't entertaining, but they are recorded in Scripture for a spiritual effect on the readers. Jesus was giving spiritual insight through these parables. That means that God was revealing himself and his truth to us through these parables.

Have you ever thought about the comparison of miracles and parables? Someone said that a miracle was the truth of God in *works*, while a parable was the truth of God in *words*. They also noted that Jesus used miracles to draw attention to a specific principle, while he used parables to explain that principle.

And by the way, there are no miraculous acts in any of the parables that Jesus taught, because his stories were about normal people in their normal life. Jesus talked about normal things so that the normal people who heard him could relate to the stories.

Now think about it: God who is infinite and unlimited in heaven—the Almighty One—condescended to communicate to his people on earth—limited and finite—by simple stories. And what do these stories communicate? They tell of the great power and wisdom of God, but more than that, they tell of his love. These parables were the best available tools Jesus could use to effectively tell people the gospel and that God loved them.

Understanding Parables

When reading a parable, don't look for hidden meanings. These are simple stories to tell eternal truth in a simple way. To understand the parable, look for the *one central truth* that each parable communicates. The parable of the Good Samaritan was introduced with a question, "Who is my neighbor?" Therefore this parable is about being a neighbor to a needy person. How do you find that point? By looking at the way Jesus introduced the parable and the way he concluded it. Look to see how much of it was interpreted by Jesus himself.

In the parable of the Good Samaritan, Jesus did not give it any special introduction; he just began telling the story, "A man was going down from Jerusalem to Jericho, when he fell into the hands of robbers." All the listeners knew the road that the man took, because there was only one road from Jerusalem to Jericho. And all of Jesus' listeners knew that it was a dangerous road, and quite often the people were robbed if they went alone. Jesus didn't interpret this parable at the beginning, but at the end. Jesus ended the story by asking the question, "Which of the these three do you think was a neighbor to the man who fell into the hands of the robbers?" This conclusion addresses the question that was raised by the lawyer in the first place: "Who is my neighbor?" By using the pronoun "you" in "Who do you think?" Jesus personalized the parable.

There are two easy mistakes to make when reading a parable. First, some people err by reading too much into a parable. For instance, in regards to the parable we've been discussing, some interpreters have said that the man who went down from Jerusalem was Adam leaving the presence of God, Jericho was the city of humanity, and the devil was the thief who beat up the man. They see the priest and the Levites as the inability of the Old Testament law to help anyone. When the Good Samaritan bound up the man's wounds, some people make that the restraint of sin, and some have even tried to make the beast on which the afflicted men rode, either Christ, or the church, or a believer. And of course some make the inn into the church.

When you try to make something of every point of a parable, it's like pressing a baseball flat to make every part of the ball touch every part of a flat plane. If you do, it's no longer a ball. When you try to see meaning in every point of a parable, it is no longer a parable. Then you usually miss the main point that Jesus was making.

The Parables of the Bible

Parables of Jesus Christ	Matthew	Mark	Luke
Jesus on Parables	13:10-35		
Parables to Disciples		4:33-34	
Lamp Under the Basket	5:14-16	4:21-22	8:16-17 11:33-36
A Wise Man Builds on Rock and A Foolish Man Builds on Sand	7:24-27		6:47-49
Unshrunk (New) Cloth on an Old Garment	9:16	2:21	5:36
New Wine in Old Wineskins	9:17	2:22	5:37-38
The Sower	13:3-23	4:2-20	8:4-15
Wheat and Tares	13:24-30		
Mustard Seed	13:31-32	4:30-32	13:18-19
The Leaven	13:33		13:20-21
Treasure in the Field	13:44		
Treasured Pearl	13:45-46		
Net	13:47-50		
Householder	13:52		
The Lost Sheep	18:12-14		15:1-7
The Unforgiving Slave	18:23-35		
The Workers in the Vineyard	20:1-16		
The Two Sons	21:28-32		
The Wicked Vinedressers	21:33-45	12:1-12	20:9-19
Wedding Feast	22:1-14		
Fig Tree	24:32-44	13:28-32	21:29-33
Man on a Long Journey		13:34-37	
Ten Virgins	25:1-13		
Talents	25:14-30		

The Parables of the Bible

Parables of Jesus Christ	Matthew	Mark	Luke
Sheep and Goats	25:31-46		
The Creditor and Two Debtors			7:41-43
Good Samaritan			10:30-37
A Friend in Need			11:5-13
The Rich Fool			12:13-21
The Faithful and the Evil Servant			12:35-40
The Faithful and Wise Steward			12:42-48
Barren Fig Tree			13:6-9
The Great Supper			14:15-24
Building a Tower and a King Making War			14:25-35
Lost Sheep			15:1-7
Lost Coin			15:8-10
Lost Son/Prodigal Son			15:11-32
The Unjust Steward			16:1-13
Lazarus and the Rich Man			16:19-31
Unprofitable Servants			17:7-10
Unjust Judge			18:1-8
Publican and the Pharisee			18:9-14
Ten Pounds			19:11-27
The Growing Seed		4:26-29	
The Absent Householder		13:33-37	

Chapter 7

Reading the Bible Devotionally

Reading the Bible devotionally is not so much a technique as it is a spirit or attitude. You must read with a spirit of eagerness to know the mind of God and what he is saying to you. You must read with a spirit of humility because God who is your Creator also wants to talk with you. You must read with a spirit of adoration, because you worship God when you come into his presence. You must read with a spirit of adventure, because you are entering a new experience in the presence of God.

We are commanded to read the Scriptures, but we shouldn't read the Bible just for that reason. Husbands are commanded to love their wives, but good ones don't do it out of obligation, but out of desire and commitment. The more you learn of a person, the more you love. So it is with the Bible. You should develop the appreciation of reading the Bible devotionally because in the Bible you will meet God, experience God, and know God intimately.

So, how can you read the Bible devotionally? Open the cover and follow your heart. Let your emotions soak up the words of Scripture. Let your heart speak to God as he speaks to you. The following are some guidelines to help you get more from the Scriptures, devotionally.

fore reading the Bible. Remember God has something say to you, and you want to hear his message so you can do what he tells you to do. Pray with the psalmist: "Open thou mine eyes, that I may behold wondrous things out of thy law" (Psalm 119:18).

2. *Choose passages that are more devotional in nature.* There are sections of Scripture better suited to devotional reading. Remember, parts of the Bible are history and genealogies, parts are systematic teaching called doctrine. Turn to the Psalms, for instance. They are concerned with experiencing God and walking with him. Other portions to read might include the Sermon on the Mount (see Matthew 5–7), the Upper Room discourse (see John 13-18), and some of the Epistles (letters) like Ephesians, Philippians, Colossians, and 1 John. The following passage is an example of the kind of reading I am talking about:

> My dear children, I write this to you so that you will not sin. But if anybody does sin, we have one who speaks to the Father in our defense—Jesus Christ, the Righteous One. He is the atoning sacrifice for our sins, and not only for ours but also for the sins of the whole world. We know that we have come to know him if we obey his commands. The man who says, "I know him," but does not do what he commands is a liar, and the truth is not in him. But if anyone obeys his word, God's love is truly made complete in him. This is how we know we are in him: Whoever claims to live in him must walk as Jesus did.
>
> 1 John 2:1-6, NIV

3. *Give yourself time to absorb the Scriptures.* Don't read devotional sections quickly, as you might read a mystery. Rather, let yourself feel the passage and listen to the words of God. You will want to read devotional passages more than once so that you might absorb the message that God is saying to you. In Deuteronomy 6:7 we read, "You shall teach them [the Scriptures] diligently to your children, and shall talk of them when you sit in your house, when you walk by the way, when you lie down, and when you rise up" (NKJV). In other words, God is showing us four times that you should be thinking and meditating on Scripture: (1) Upon waking each morning, (2) Before going to sleep each evening, (3) While going from place to place, (4) When you sit or wait.

4. *Ask yourself some heart questions as you read.* As you read the Bible devotionally, these questions will help you think and apply the message to your heart.

- What is God saying in this passage?
- What do I feel when God speaks?
- What does God want me to know, to feel, to become?
- What can I learn about God in this passage?

As you read a passage, does it tell you what God will do for you in times of trouble? Does it tell you how to react to God? As you review the passage, look for principles to become a deeper Christian. Don't forget your feelings. How were your emotions stirred as you read the passage? Do you want to do more for God? Since we are talking about devotions, what did you learn about worship in this Scripture, and how will you worship God now that you have finished reading it?

5. *Find the key verse in devotional Scripture.* A key verse is the one that holds the passage together. Usually a key verse jumps out at you as you read the passage. You will want to underline or highlight it. A doctrinal key verse (see chapter ten) helps you interpret a passage, but a devotional key verse helps you feel the passage and apply it to your life.

If you sit down at someone's computer, you can't make heads or tails until you find the key to activate the screen. In the same way, the key devotional verse that activates the chapter is more felt than explained. The key verse will help make the message of God appear on the screen of your mind.

A key verse will do two things for you. First, it will summarize the essence of what God is saying in the chapter. Second, a key verse is pivotal in relating to the rest of the Bible. To illustrate, read the verses from Ephesians 2 below. The first part reminds the readers of all that God has done to make their salvation possible. Then comes the key verse (in italics). The last part reminds readers that their new life in Christ is like God's project, his "workmanship."

> But God, who is rich in mercy, because of His great love with which He loved us, even when we were dead in trespasses, made us alive together with Christ (by grace you have been saved), and raised us up together, and made us sit together in the heavenly places in Christ Jesus, that in the ages to come He might show the exceeding riches of His grace in His kindness toward us in Christ Jesus. *For by grace you have been saved through faith, and that not of yourselves; it is the gift of God, not of works, lest anyone should boast.* For we are His workmanship, created in

> Christ Jesus for good works, which God prepared beforehand that we should walk in them.
>
> EPHESIANS 2:4-10, NKJV (emphasis added)

6. *Look for key words in the devotional passage.* A key verse and a key word are different, even though the key word may be found in the key verse. As you read over the passage two or three times, underline or highlight the word that opens up the passage to you. You can find which words are the important ones by asking yourself the following questions:

- What word appears most often?
- What word applies the passage to my life?
- How does the writer use this word?
- What does this word mean to you today, as compared to what it meant in the Bible?
- What does this word reveal about God, people, sin or salvation?
- How does this word help you live a stronger Christian life?

For example, one of the key words to understand 1 Corinthians 13 is *love.* As you read the following passage, underline the word *love.* I've used the Living Bible paraphrase because the old King James Version translated *love* with the word "charity."

> If I had the gift of being able to speak in other languages without learning them, and could speak in every language there is in all of heaven and earth, but didn't *love* others, I would only be making noise. If I had the gift of prophecy and knew all about what is going to happen in the future, knew everything about *everything,* but didn't *love* others,

what good would it do? Even if I had the gift of faith so that I could speak to a mountain and make it move, I would still be worth nothing at all without *love.* If I gave everything I have to poor people, and if I were burned alive for preaching the Gospel but didn't *love* others, it would be of no value whatever.

Love is very patient and kind, never jealous or envious, never boastful or proud, never haughty or selfish or rude. *Love* does not demand its own way. It is not irritable or touchy. It does not hold grudges and will hardly even notice when others do it wrong. It is never glad about injustice, but rejoices whenever truth wins out. If you *love* someone you will be loyal to him no matter what the cost. You will always believe in him, always expect the best of him, and always stand your ground in defending him.

All the special gifts and powers from God will someday come to end, but *love* goes on forever. Someday prophecy, and speaking in unknown languages, and special knowledge—these gifts will disappear. Now we know so little, even with our special gifts, and the preaching of those most gifted is still so poor. But when we have been made perfect and complete, then the need for these in-adequate special gifts will come to an end, and they will disappear.

It's like this: when I was a child I spoke and thought and reasoned as a child does. But when I became a man my thoughts grew far beyond those of my childhood, and now I have put away the childish things. In the same way, we can see and understand only a little about God now, as if we were peering at his reflection in a poor mirror; but someday we are going to see him in his completeness, face to face. Now all that I know is hazy and blurred, but then I will see everything clearly, just as clearly as God sees into my heart right now.

There are three things that remain—faith, hope, and *love*—and the greatest of these is *love.*

1 CORINTHIANS 13:1-13, LB (emphasis added)

7. *Look for things that specifically relate to walking with Christ.* As you read a passage devotionally, look for those things that relate to your living for Christ. If the passage is a testimony by another person, you can ask yourself the question, "Can I use these same principles in my life?" If the passage is a conversation, or part of a letter written by Paul, you can ask yourself, "What are they suggesting?" It's easy to find the personal application if you're reading a promise from God, a prayer to pray, or an exhortation to obey.

You might ask yourself these questions:

- Is there an example to follow?
- Is there an exhortation to obey?
- Is there a sin to avoid?
- Is there a responsibility to fulfill?
- Is there a promise to claim?
- Is there a prayer to pray?

As you read the Bible devotionally, expect to find the following:

- Promises to claim.
- Examples to follow.
- Habits to forsake.
- Sins to confess.

- Commands to obey.
- Attitudes to imitate.
- Actions to experience.
- Truths to believe.

8. *Use common sense when applying the Scriptures to your life.* You should realize that many things will not apply to you directly. A student that I met while attending Bible college in South Carolina was from New York State. He gave the testimony that God led him down to South Carolina when he read the command of God to the prophet, "Go south..." I'd say that's an illustration of a wrong application of Scripture.

Common sense tells you the difference between what the Bible is *dictating* and what it is *describing*. As an illustration, the Bible describes Abraham having a child by one of his servant girls because his wife thought she was too old to have a child. The Bible describes what Abraham did, but it does not tell us to follow this example. You should not follow this practice of having sex outside your marriage vow. A related point: watch for both positive and negative examples in Scriptures. Samson was an esteemed judge of Israel but he was also unwise in his relationship to women. You should not follow his example of adultery.

Common sense tells us that some commands were given historically to individuals, but we are not to obey the command today. Jesus told his disciples to "tarry" in Jerusalem and pray. That does not mean we should go to Jerusalem to pray nor does it mean that we always need to wait through days of prayer meetings before getting answers.

Common sense should help you distinguish between cultural expressions and eternal principles. In the culture of Bible times, a Nazarite made a promise to God and sealed his oath by growing his beard and long hair. Obviously, that is not a command for us today—especially for women!

Again, common sense tells us that not every promise that God made in the Bible applies to our personal life today. On Resurrection morning, Jesus told the women to instruct the disciples to go into Galilee, "There shall they see me" (Matthew 28:10). That promise does not mean we should try to see Jesus in Galilee today. That promise was for select people for a select time.

Common sense tells us that some promises are conditional, while others are unconditional. When Jesus promised that if we ask anything in his name, he will do it (see John 14:14), some people think that no matter their spiritual condition, they can pray for anything, anytime, and they'll get it. But, the conditional promise is to ask in Jesus' name. Notice the "if," which means we must pray in Jesus' name, obeying all the conditions that are implied in walking in fellowship with him. Those conditions including being separated from sin and praying within the will of God. There are a lot of prayers that are not answered because people don't meet the conditions. Watch for conditional language when reading the Bible.

Reading the Bible devotionally is the way most people read the Bible. Since you're looking for spiritual help, then follow the principles of this chapter to become a better Christian as a result of your reading.

CHAPTER 8

READING THE BIBLE—ONE BOOK AT A TIME

The Bible is a big book. Actually, it is a collection of sixty-six books containing 1,189 chapters, 31,175 verses. When reading a book as big as the Bible, it is best to begin with a plan. Since Scripture was originally written as individual books and letters, focus on reading each book of the Bible, one book at a time. Many people find that if you concentrate your reading on a book-by-book plan, you will gain a better understanding of Scripture. There are other plans or approaches to Bible reading, (such as reading chronologically, or reading from the Old Testament in the morning and the New Testament in the evening). But this chapter suggests staying with one book of the Bible at a time to help you understand the original message of Scripture. Ultimately, the whole Bible will unfold for you as you master one book at a time.

Even reading just one of the sixty-six books of the Bible can be a challenging task. Several books contain more than thirty chapters. If we read a chapter a day, it would take more than a month to read these books. However, some books contain only a few chapters.

The first step in reading a book of the Bible is to gain a broad understanding of it as a whole. Later, you can examine the parts of the book in greater detail. Set aside time to read through the entire book without interruption. After completing this reading, jot down any immediate impressions. What is the author saying? What is the theme of the book in one sentence? What is unique about the way the author says things? What kind of feel did you get from the book?

Once you have recorded your first impressions, take time to read the book again. Read it in light of your theme sentence. This time, look for a sense of order in the book. Most authors develop their themes in different ways in different parts of a book. Divide the book into parts. How do they fit into the overall theme? Is there a particular verse or passage that might be viewed as a key to understanding the book? Underline the verse or highlight the passage for easy reference.

Each time you read a book, you gain more understanding of it. As you reread a book, take time to write a brief title for each chapter. You can write this on a separate piece of paper, or in the margins of your Bible. Titling each chapter will help you pick up additional details in the book. You may wish to read through the book again, looking at it from a different perspective on each occasion. You might consider key people, principles emphasized, ideas proposed, geography, or unique expressions repeated throughout the book.

After reading through the book several times, try summarizing your observations in a one-page outline. You will have to be selective in what you choose to include and leave out. Try to identify each main division and subdivision in the book. This outline will be the skeleton upon which you will build the rest of your reading.

Five Steps in Personal Bible Reading

Now that you have an understanding of the book as a whole, begin looking at each paragraph in greater detail. The paragraph is the basic unit of thought in writing. As you examine each paragraph, ask questions about what you are reading: who, what, when, where, and why?

The first question relating to observation is the "Who" question. Read the text carefully to determine who is mentioned in the book. Use questions journalists might use to learn details about a news story. As you make observations, write them down on paper. It has been well said that the shortest pencil is better than the longest memory.

Your second question relates to interpretation, or the "What" question. What does this passage mean? At this point, you may want to consult a Bible commentary or other resource to look up the meaning of certain passages. You will consult a Bible dictionary to understand words, expressions, backgrounds, or events.

The third question is one of time perspective, or the "When" question. When did the events take place? What else was happening at the same time? How does your reading fit in with what the Bible says in other places? Truth always exists in balance. Sometimes a statement in one verse is better understood when related to a statement in some other verse.

The fourth question relates to location; it is the "Where" question. Where does the action take place? Again, you will want to consult a Bible dictionary to discuss the historical, geographical, and spiritual background of the places about which you read. When you understand the geographical context, you better understand the action and conversations in a paragraph.

The final question you need to ask in your Bible reading is the "Why" question. What difference is your reading going to make in your life? God wants you to be doers as well as hearers or students of Scripture (see James 1:22). What steps are involved in assimilating this principle in your life? Then, how can you best share these principles with others? The Bible tells us we are to teach one another (see Colossians 3:16). Just as the principles you learn in your Bible reading help you grow, so you can help others experience growth by sharing what you are learning with them.

Getting Started in Bible Reading

Simply knowing how to read the Bible is not enough. The real benefits of personal Bible reading are not yours until you begin. If you are not already engaged in the systematic reading of the Bible, choose a Bible book and begin today. The average reader could read through any one of these books in less than half an hour. When you come to things you don't understand, don't get discouraged. Concentrate on what you do understand and learn from that first. You will find that what you do understand, will eventually help you with what you don't understand.

When you approach Bible reading, you are listening to a message from God. Therefore, as you begin your reading of a book, be sure you are prepared to hear what God is saying in that book. Ask God to open your eyes and give you insight into what you read (see Psalm 119:18). If the book tells of sin, and you have sin hindering your relationship with God, then confess it to him and seek cleansing (see 1 John 1:9). As you read, listen to what God is saying to you (see 1 Samuel 3:10). Is he saying something to you personally? To you now? Be prepared to do what God tells you through your personal Bible encounters (see Acts 9:6).

Does it seem like a lot is involved in just reading the Bible? Perhaps so, but the more you invest in personal Bible reading, the greater the return. Be careful not to shortchange yourself by approaching the Bible with a shallow attitude. As you grow in your understanding of the Scriptures, you may want to try other approaches to Bible reading, such as concentrating on devotional aspects, or prophecies, or doctrine.

Chapter 9

Reading Prophecy in the Bible

As you read the Bible, you will find prophecies of coming events and people who will live in the future. God has written into Scripture some glimpses of future happenings. This should increase your confidence in the message of the Word.

Prophecy has done more to demonstrate that God wrote the Bible than any other argument. Why? Because no other religion can demonstrate that its leader's coming to earth and ministry was predicted before he was born—not Buddhism, not Confucianism, not Islam; none of them.

Predictions About Jesus

Let's briefly survey some of the predictions about Jesus that were made before he was born. Some critics say prophecy doesn't prove anything because the predictions could be planted in the text after the fact. But the discovery of the Dead Sea Scrolls demonstrates these passages were written long before they happened:

- The Bible predicted the Savior's mother would be a virgin. "Behold a virgin shall conceive ... a Son, and shall call His name Immanuel (*God with us*) (Isaiah 7:14, NKJV, parentheses added).
- The Bible foretold where Jesus would be born: "But you, Bethlehem Ephrathah, though you are little among the thousands of Judah, yet out of you shall come forth to Me the One to be Ruler in Israel, whose goings forth are from of old, from everlasting" (Micah 5:2, NKJV).
- Even though some deny the deity of Jesus, the Bible said this about him: "For unto us a child is born, unto us a son is given: and the government shall be upon his shoulder: and his name shall be called Wonderful, Counsellor, The mighty God, The everlasting Father, The Prince of Peace (Isaiah 9:6).
- The Bible predicted his ministry of preaching, miracles, and compassion. "The Spirit of the Lord God is upon me (Jesus); because the Lord hath anointed me to preach good tidings unto the meek; he hath sent me to bind up the brokenhearted, to proclaim liberty to the captives, and the opening of the prison to them that are bound; to proclaim the acceptable year of the Lord" (Isaiah 61:1-2, parentheses added).
- His triumphant entry into Jerusalem was foretold, even including the detail that Jesus would ride into the city on a donkey. "Shout, O daughter of Jerusalem: behold, thy King cometh unto thee: he is just, and having salvation; lowly, and riding upon an ass, and upon a colt the foal of an ass" (Zechariah 9:9).
- His betrayal was predicted, including the price paid to Judas. "So they weighed for my price thirty pieces of silver" (Zechariah 11:12).

- His agony and words from the cross were foretold: "My God, my God, why hast thou forsaken me?" (Psalm 22:1)
- Also his substitutionary death: "The Lord hath laid on him the iniquity of us all" (Isaiah 53:6).
- And his resurrection: "For thou wilt not leave my soul in hell; neither wilt thou suffer thine Holy One to see corruption" (Psalm 16:10).
- As well as his ascension into heaven: "The Lord said unto my Lord, 'Sit thou on my right hand, till I make thine enemies thy footstool?'" (Matthew 22:44).

No one knows the future but God. He knows all things, including the events of tomorrow and the distant future. Those who have claimed to predict the future have had a high degree of errors in their predictions. They are only guessing. However, the predictions about Jesus were all made at least four hundred years before he lived, and some of them were predicted over a thousand years before he was born. And since all the predictions about Jesus are accurate, we must assume that only God could have written the Bible, because only God knows the future. Therefore, as you are reading the Bible, watch for Old Testament predictions about Jesus Christ, mark your Bible, and gain confidence from these anchors.

Interpretations of Prophecy

But as mentioned earlier, there is a problem with reading prophecy. Many have read the Bible and made wrong predictions about the future. For example, many have identified certain leaders during their era as the Antichrist, a person identified in the Bible as a coming world ruler. In the late 1930s, a radio evangelist said Benito Mussolini was the Antichrist because Mussolini was from Italy, the region many think will be the origin of the Antichrist. In the 1970s, another radio preacher identified former U.S. secretary of state Henry Kissinger as the Antichrist because Kissinger supported the unification of the nations of Europe, just as the Antichrist is predicted to reunify a revived Roman Empire. When Kissinger was spotted in a limousine with the license plates 666—the number associated with the Antichrist—that only reinforced the interpretation. Someone else predicted that John Lennon of the Beatles was the Antichrist because he was corrupting the young people. The same thing had been said earlier about Elvis Presley.

In 1988, a television preacher published and mailed a small book to over a million homes in the United States claiming "88 reasons why the Rapture would come in 1988." He was wrong. In South Korea, a leader announced that the Lord was coming, convincing all his followers to sell their property and goods, to get ready for the coming of Jesus. He, too, was wrong, and later imprisoned for making illegal money by purchasing the pro-perty of church members.

Because of the many and varied mistakes about prophecy, some people just won't read any books that have to do with it. Because of this narrow opinion, some have never read the wonderful books of Revelation, Zechariah, or Daniel.

More than one third of the Bible was prophetic when written, so you can't get away from prophecy if you're going to read the entire Bible, which of course you should. Think of all the Old Testament prophecies that talked about the coming kingdoms of the world, such as the book of Daniel. Young Daniel interpreted a dream of Nebuchadnezzar that predicted four coming world empires. If you've never read this prophecy, examine it carefully, because history has revealed the accuracy of this prophecy (see Daniel 2:31-45).

THE PREDICTIVE DREAM OF NEBUCHADNEZZAR

Kingdom	**Empire**	**Emperor**
The kingdom of gold	Babylon	Nebuchadnezzar
The divided kingdom of silver	Media-Persia	Cyrus
The third kingdom of brass	Greece	Alexander the Great
The fourth kingdom of iron	Rome	Caesar

When the Dead Sea Scrolls were found, they verified the prediction because they indicated the book of Daniel was written before the final two kingdoms came into existence. There was no indication these nations would become world powers when the prophecy was given.

> O, king, (Nebuchadnezzar), you saw a huge and powerful statue of a man, shining brilliantly, frightening and terrible. The head of the statue was made of purest gold, its chest and arms were of silver, its belly and thighs of brass, its legs of iron, its feet part iron and part clay. But as you watched, a Rock was cut from the mountainside by supernatural means. It came hurtling toward the statue and crushed the feet of iron and clay, smashing them into bits. Then the whole statue collapsed into a heap of iron, clay, brass, silver, and gold; its pieces were crushed as small as chaff, and the wind blew them all away. But the Rock that knocked

the statue down became a great mountain that covered the whole earth. That was the dream; now for its meaning: Your Majesty, you are a king over many kings, for the God of heaven has given you your kingdom, power, strength and glory. You rule the farthest provinces, and even animals and birds are under your control, as God decreed. You are that head of gold. But after your kingdom has come to an end, another world power will arise to take your place. This empire will be inferior to yours. And after that kingdom has fallen, yet a third great power—represented by the bronze belly of the statue—will rise to rule the world. Following it, the fourth kingdom will be strong as iron—smashing, bruising, and conquering. The feet and toes you saw—part iron and part clay—show that later on, this kingdom will be divided. Some parts of it will be as strong as iron, and some as weak as clay. This mixture of iron with clay also shows that these kingdoms will try to strengthen themselves by forming alliances with each other through intermarriage of their rulers; but this will not succeed, for iron and clay don't mix. During the reigns of those kings, the God of heaven will set up a kingdom that will never be destroyed; no one will ever conquer it. It will shatter all these kingdoms into nothingness, but it shall stand forever, indestructible. That is the meaning of the Rock cut from the mountain without human hands—the Rock that crushed to powder all the iron and brass, the clay, the silver, and the gold.

DANIEL 2:31-45, LB

As you read prophecy, keep your mind wide open to learn

truth. Don't jump quickly to conclusions, but gather all the facts of the Bible before indicating a prediction has been fulfilled. Remember, for instance, that anyone predicting the second coming of Jesus Christ will be wrong. Why do we know that? Because Jesus said only the Father knows that day and hour (see Matthew 24:36). Martin Luther is reported to have said, "If anyone correctly guesses when Jesus will return, the Father will change the date, because the Scriptures tell us no one knows."

If you have not read prophecy, you have missed a special blessing that God has for you. "Blessed is he who reads and those who hear the words of this prophecy, and keep those things which are written in it; for the time is near" (Revelation 1:3, NKJV).

When Paul planted the church at Thessalonica, even though he preached there only "three Sabbath days" (see Acts 17:2), he instructed them in prophecy. He taught them to expect the return of Christ at any moment and what the world would be like when Jesus returned. Notice Paul didn't wait a long time for them to grow in Christian maturity before teaching prophecy. As a result, the Thessalonians had some questions after Paul left, and he needed to answer them by writing letters. The Thessalonians wanted to know if Christians who died before the return of the Lord Jesus would be caught up when Jesus came. Paul wrote,

> But I do not want you to be ignorant, brethren, concerning those who have fallen asleep, lest you sorrow as others who have no hope. For if we believe that Jesus died and rose again, so also God will bring with Him those who sleep in Jesus. For this we say to you by the word of the

> Lord, that we who are alive and remain until the coming of the Lord will by no means precede those who are asleep. For the Lord Himself will descend from heaven with a shout, with the voice of an archangel, and with the trumpet of God. And the dead in Christ will rise first. Then we who are alive and remain shall be caught up together with them in the clouds to meet the Lord in the air. And thus we shall always be with the Lord.
>
> 1 THESSALONIANS 4:13-17, NKJV

When reading prophecy you will not understand everything, because you don't have the background, nor do you know the conditions when prophecy was written. Also, God will not tell us everything about some predictions. Therefore, don't jump to conclusions because you don't have all the facts.

> The secret things belong to the Lord our God, but the things revealed belong to us and to our children forever, that we may follow all the words of this law.
>
> DEUTERONOMY 29:29, NIV

After Paul wrote the first Epistle (letter) to the Thessalonians to explain that the dead would be caught up with the living when Jesus returned, the Thessalonian believers had another problem. Because they were suffering persecution from people who hated Christ, they thought their tribulation was a signal that the world was coming to an end. Specifically, they wanted to know if Jesus had already come and they had missed it. To answer this misunderstanding, Paul wrote a second letter to the Thessalonians.

And now, what about the coming again of our Lord Jesus Christ, and our being gathered together to meet him? Please don't be upset and excited, dear brothers, by the rumor that this day of the Lord has already begun. If you hear of people having visions and special messages from God about this, or letters that are supposed to have come from me, don't believe them. Don't be carried away and deceived regardless of what they say.

For that day will not come until two things happen: first, there will be a time of great rebellion against God, and then the man of rebellion will come—the son of hell. He will defy every god there is, and tear down every other object of adoration and worship. He will go in and sit as God in the temple of God, claiming that he himself is God. Don't you remember that I told you this when I was with you? And you know this when I was with you? And you know what is keeping him from being here already; for he can come only when his time is ready.

As for the work this man of rebellion and hell will do when he comes, it is already going on, but he himself will not come until the one who is holding him back steps out of the way. Then this wicked one will appear, whom the Lord Jesus will burn up with the breath of his mouth and destroy by his presence when he returns. This man of sin will come as Satan's tool, full of satanic power, and will trick everyone with strange demonstrations, and will do great miracles. He will completely fool those who are on their way to hell because they have said "no" to the Truth; they have refused to believe it and love it, and let it save them, so God will allow them to believe lies with all their hearts.

2 THESSALONIANS 2:1-11, LB

Don't get hung up on difficult passages about prophecy. Take them by faith, knowing God is in control and all things will work out to his glory. Just be concerned about prophecies that you understand and those that relate to you. Take heaven, for example. It is a real place, where real people will spend a real eternity. When Jesus used the phrase, "My Father's house" to refer to heaven, he was predicting all believers would go into God's presence at death (see John 14:2-4).

What can you learn from this prediction? First, Jesus is telling us that he is preparing a place for us within the Father's home. Second, Jesus will return to receive us to himself at the Rapture or at our death. Third, we will spend eternity with Jesus and with the Father in heaven.

Primary Focus

There is another principle for reading prophecy. Don't focus primarily on things or objects such as marching armies, a beast arising out of the sea, or hailstones. The focal point of the future is not about things like the Battle of Armageddon or the river of God that comes out of the Throne of God. Everything in prophecy focuses on the Lord Jesus Christ. When you come to Revelation, the greatest book on prophecy, notice how it is introduced, "The Revelation of Jesus Christ" (see Revelation 1:1). It is about Jesus Christ. So when you read the first chapter of Revelation, underline all the different names for Jesus. When you see his many names, then you'll understand his divine nature and what he's coming to do for us. Then you'll fall on your face to worship as did John. "And when I saw him,

I fell at his feet as dead. And he laid his right hand upon me, saying unto me, Fear not; I am the first and the last" (Revelation 1:17).

Read prophecy and enjoy yourself. After decades of reading, I still do. Read prophecy even though you don't understand everything. I sure don't. Read prophecy to fill in the missing pieces of God's future plan. I'm still learning. Let's read prophecy to grow in grace and learn more about our wonderful Lord who said at the end of the Bible, "Surely I come quickly" (Revelation 22:20).

Chapter 10

Reading the Bible Doctrinally

The great evangelist Dwight L. Moody didn't like to study doctrine, he just wanted to study the Bible. He once said, "Feeding on doctrine is like trying to live on dry husks, every farmer knows that the husks will not put fat on the cattle, or meat on the bones." Moody was reacting to the "dead" doctrine he saw in many dead churches.

Anytime anyone takes several verses and synthesizes them into one Sunday school lesson, he is constructing doctrine. Even Moody, when he took several references to Jesus Christ, and put them together into one sermon, was constructing a doctrine of Jesus. So, don't be afraid of the word "doctrine."

Yet someone once said, "No creed but Christ!" That cryptic slogan may be correct, but it could be misleading. The problem is, what do you mean when you say "Jesus Christ"? To some people, Jesus Christ is only a good man. They look to the life of Jesus Christ, but miss what he said about himself. He claimed deity—in other words, he said he was God himself. "I and the Father are one," he said, and "Anyone who has seen me has seen the Father" (see John 10:30, 14:9, NIV). So, to have biblical doctrine about Jesus Christ you must include everything that is included about him in the Word of God.

But some people still miss the point. They refuse to recognize that Jesus was born of a virgin (see Matthew 1:18-23) and they will not confess that he lived a sinless life (see 1 Peter 2:21-22). These same people may say that Jesus died a martyr's death on the cross, not admitting that he was the substitute for all sinners (see 2 Corinthians 5:21). They may refuse to believe that Jesus took away the sin of the world (see John 1:29). They believe in a humanistic Jesus; therefore, they have a humanistic doctrine.

Moody understood that the cohesive glue holding doctrine together was Jesus. The glue wasn't logic or people's ability to put things together. Moody said, "Doctrine is like a road or a street, it is only as good as it takes you some place. But if it doesn't take you to Christ, it's worthless."

Certain books of the Bible include more doctrine than others. These would include Romans, Galatians, and Hebrews. When you read Bible doctrine, you are doing the same thing Christians did in the early church. "And they continued steadfastly in the apostles' doctrine and fellowship, and in breaking of bread, and in prayers" (Acts 2:42).

But reading doctrine may be difficult or, at best, not much fun. This chapter should help you learn how to read doctrine and get more out of it. Remember, though, that God has written all the Bible to you. Because it is a message from him, you'll want to read it all—including types of literature that might be drier than others.

First, let's look at exactly what doctrine is. Simply speaking, the English word doctrine comes from the Latin term for teaching. When you teach a lesson, you use the verb *indoctrinate* to explain your ideas. But when a student writes down the lessons learned, it is the noun ***doctrine.*** Indoctrinate is the ***verb,*** doctrine is the ***noun.***

Our doctrine is the things we believe about God and salvation. There is correct doctrine—what the Bible teaches—and false doctrine—that which is contrary to the Bible. Notice Paul tells us there is false doctrine to avoid, so that "...we should no longer be children, tossed to and fro and carried about with every wind of doctrine, by the trickery of men, in the cunning craftiness by which they lie in wait to deceive" (Ephesians 4:14, NKJV). Instead correct doctrine comes from the Bible: "All Scripture is given by inspiration of God and is profitable for doctrine..." (2 Timothy 3:16).

Let's move to a second important point. The Bible was not written in doctrinal format, but rather is a record of how God related to people in their struggle to find him. The Bible contains stories of God speaking, guiding, intervening in circumstances, and doing miracles through men and women of God. All these events are written in the Bible. As you read these events and put it together, you understand the patterns by which God works and the principles he follows. Patterns and principles are the laws of God by which he operates. When you put all these things together, that's another way of saying you put doctrine together.

Jesus told us how to determine correct doctrine, when he said, "My doctrine is not Mine, but His who sent Me. If anyone wants to do His will, he shall know concerning the doctrine, whether it is from God or whether I speak on My own authority" (John 7:16-17, NKJV). Notice two things about this verse. First, Jesus was explaining the way God communicated his principles, calling it doctrine. Second, we can understand

God's principles—doctrine—if we really search God's principles and are willing to accept what God says.

At the end of the Sermon on the Mount, for instance, the people marveled at the doctrine of Jesus, "And they were all amazed, so that they questioned among themselves, saying, 'What is this? What new doctrine is this? For with authority He commands even the unclean spirits, and they obey him'" (Mark 1:27, NKJV). The crowd was skeptical that Jesus was casting out demons. The people called it "a new doctrine," which was their explanation of the way things were done. But the actions of Jesus backing up by his words couldn't be denied.

When you read doctrine, remember this is where God explains the meaning behind the actions. Doctrine will be easier to understand when you look for God, rather than looking for a doctrinal statement. You must believe in his existence, as you try to determine his nature and actions, "But without faith it is impossible to please Him, for he who comes to God must believe that he is, and that he is a rewarder of those who diligently seek him" (Hebrews 11:6, NKJV). This means you must have faith in God to understand the Bible.

As you approach the study of any doctrine, begin making a list of all the biblical passages that relate to your topic. You will want to take several steps in compiling this list. First, search a concordance for key words relating to that doctrine. Next, consult a good topical Bible under the heading of the doctrine you are considering. Many reference Bibles include cross-references designed to lead the reader through a study of biblical topics.

Once the list has been compiled, read each passage and make your own brief notes concerning the topic. Remember, the study of a biblical doctrine is built on certain presuppositions.

First, your doctrine should be based on the literal interpretation of the Bible. Second, your doctrine should be limited to the Scriptures themselves. Every effort should be made to avoid building doctrinal principles on speculative writings of people or "fancy" ideas that appeal to your imagination.

Next, arrange your basic doctrinal principles in a logical order. You should treat the topic with the same importance that people in the Bible treated it. Sometimes, it may be helpful to trace doctrinal content in chronological development. Using this approach, you need to understand Moses in order to understand Paul's interpretation of the same doctrine. Occasionally, you may want to highlight and arrange doctrinal emphasis by various biblical writers or biblical books. A doctrinal study of the church could be arranged to illustrate the unique emphases of Jesus, Peter and Paul.

When you arrange your conclusions, take time to look over the contents. Here is where you harmonize any apparent contradictions. If a conflict remains, there are a couple of principles that will help you resolve it. First, where two verses appear to say different things, the last verse written probably has the fuller revelation of that truth. Give priority to the New Testament over the Old Testament. Second, where one verse appears to say something different than several others, the consistent teaching of *many verses* is preferred over an interpretation of just *one verse*. Perhaps, there is something about the context of a verse that may explain why it is expressed that way. By checking the context more closely, the problem with the verse often disappears.

EPILOGUE

WHEN YOU COME TO THE LAST CHAPTER

When you have read the Bible all the way through—all 1,189 chapters—you will have done something that most Christians haven't done. How will it feel? Your feelings will probably match the effort you put into the project.

If you have read the Bible to obey God, you should feel trustworthy because you've done what he has asked. If you've read the Bible to learn, you should feel informed. If you've read the Bible to better know God, you should feel more spiritual than when you began.

Whatever the reason—congratulations!

No matter what happens in the future, you will always know, "I've read the Bible all the way through." However, don't let that knowledge go to your head. I once was talking to a pastor who had been "kicked out" of his church group because they accused him of heresy. That means his denomination decided he had beliefs contrary to the Bible. The pastor was indignant. "How could they do that; I've read the Bible through 107 times," he told me.

I thought about it for a minute, but didn't respond. I have not kept count, but I probably have read the Bible through that many times in my life because I had been a Christian about fifty years when that conversation happened.

I thought: if a man can read the Bible 107 times, yet still have his denomination decide he's a heretic, then the issue is not how many times you've been through the Bible, but how many times the Bible has been through you.

If you've read the Bible all the way through, you might do something I do; sign it. Inside the front cover of several of my Bibles, you'll find the statement, *I read this all the way through.* Then I sign and date it.

If you've read the Bible all the way through, determine to do it again. However, this time build on your last trip through. Whatever you've done the first time, here are a few subtle changes that will add meaning and a challenge to your next trip through the Bible.

- Read in a different version.
- Underline different things from the first time through.
- Use a different color pen or highlighter to mark your Bible.
- Underline all the different names of God.
- Follow a different reading sequence of books.
- Look for the key word of every book, underline it each time it occurs, and write it at the front of each book.
- Use a different color pen to underline a promise, a prophecy, a warning, and a command.
- Read a reference Bible, including all footnotes.

But suppose you've not read the last chapter of the Bible, although you've just come to the last chapter of this book. Okay. I have some suggestions for you.

Make a commitment to read the Bible all the way through. If you made that commitment before and didn't keep it, I can help you this time. Also, the following will help those people who have a difficult time keeping their promises, like those who can't keep their New Year's resolutions. Here are a few steps for promise-makers. First, write your commitment in the front of your Bible. Second, tell a friend about your promise, and ask them to check up on your progress. Third, follow the Bible reading plan in this book, and make a written checklist of your daily progress. Fourth, see if you can get a friend to read the same sequences with you. (You can encourage each other along the way). Fifth, if you miss a day or two, try to catch up on the weekend. Sixth, let me know about it. When you commit yourself to read the whole Bible, e-mail me at etowns@elmertowns.com. Then let me know when you've completed the task!

Now that you've finished this book, don't let it gather dust on your shelf. Sign the inside book cover, "I've read this book," then pass it on to someone who should read the Bible all the way through. The publisher might not like it because they'll lose sales; but wouldn't it be great if five more people read this book and were motivated to read the Bible all the way through? That would be worth the price you've paid for this book.

Let's do it.

APPENDIX 1

BIBLE STUDY HELPS

1. *Concordance.* This is a study tool that gives all the words in the Bible in alphabetical order. Then each word is listed as they occur in the Bible. You will use this tool to: (a) find the occurrence of a verse as it appears in the Bible when you know a few words but you don't know the reference; (b) study specific words in different settings; (c) find another verse that uses the same words; (d) find another verse with the same meaning; and (e) to study various words in their settings.

For example:
Strong, James, ed. *The New Strong's Exhaustive Concordance of the Bible.* Nashville, Tenn.: Thomas Nelson, 1997.

Internet addresses for concordances for the following Bible versions: KJV, NIV, NASB, RNKJV and others.
http://www.btinternet.com/~markolus/search1.htm
http://www.eliyah.com/lexicon.html
http://bible.crosswalk.com/Concordances/
http://www.gospelcom.net/narramore/concordance.htm

2. *Bible Dictionary.* This is a study tool that explains people, places, things, and events of the Bible, and gives the definition of words. Some include items normally found in encyclopedias.

For example:

Lockyer, Herbert, Sr., gen. ed. *Nelson Illustrated Bible Dictionary.* Nashville, Tenn.: Thomas Nelson, 1986.

http://www.umich.edu/~ivcf/Resources/dictionaries.html
http://www.gospelcom.net/apologeticsindex/b43.html

3. *Maps.* Many Bibles include maps helpful in study. These maps usually cover periods of Bible times chronologically. However, a book of maps will be more complete. Make sure to get a volume that has date-related maps, because the names of some places change over time, and some locations in one age completely disappear in another time.

For example:

Beitzel, Barry J. *The Moody Atlas of Bible Lands.* Chicago: Moody Press, 1985.

Frank, Harry Thomas, ed. *Atlas of the Bible Lands.* Rev. ed. Maplewood, N.J.: Hammond Incorporated, 1990.

May, Herbert G., ed. *Oxford Bible Atlas.* 3rd ed. New York: Oxford University Press, 1984.

http://www.biblestudy.org/maps/main.html

4. *Commentaries.* Commentaries also explain the background of places, people, and events, plus explain apparent contradictions

in Scripture. The main purpose of a commentary is to give the interpretation of a passage, in other words, what the author means to say. This can be helpful because some verses have obscure meanings, or contemporary readers may not understand the meaning of a passage because of different cultures, a change in the meaning of words, or other problems. Sometimes metaphorical language needs interpretation.

For example:

Hindson, Edward E., Woodrow Kroll, gen. eds. *The Complete Bible Commentary.* Nashville, Tenn.: Thomas Nelson, 2000.

Church, Leslie F., ed. *Matthew Henry's Commentary.* Grand Rapids, Mich.: Zondervan, 1982.

http://www.christiansunite.com/resources/commentary.shtml

The above commentaries are mentioned because they are one-volume commentaries that are affordable for most people. However, extensive commentaries are available that explain passages from the Hebrew or Greek languages. These are used primarily by ministers and teachers. It is not the purpose of this volume to include these.

Also, there are single volume commentaries available that relate to just one book in the Bible (or just a few books). These are usually more extensive in detail and explanation. With time, you will want to add some commentaries to your collection, especially those that will help you understand Bible books that you read most often; or a commentary of a book of the Bible that you might be teaching in a church Bible study.

Commentaries are written from the viewpoint of the author.

Ask your pastor to recommend a commentary that reflects your church's position. However, don't be afraid to read commentaries from other positions to get a variety of meanings and interpretations. You will be "stretched" in your understanding and will grow in Bible skills.

5. *Bible Handbook.* This is a useful tool that gives the basic information about each book in the Bible, such as the author, time of writing, dates, theme, key words, conditions, or motivation for writing. A Bible handbook also contains a summary of each chapter and other pertinent information about the Bible.

For example:

Halley, Henry H. *Halley's Bible Handbook.* Grand Rapids, Mich.: Zondervan, 1976.

Willmington, Harold L. *Willmington Bible Handbook.* Wheaton, Ill.: Tyndale House, 1997.

Appendix 2

Daily Bible Reading Schedule

JANUARY

[_] 1 Genesis 1-3
[_] 2 Genesis 4-7
[_] 3 Genesis 8-11
[_] 4 Genesis 12-15
[_] 5 Genesis 16-18
[_] 6 Genesis 19-20
[_] 7 Genesis 21-23
[_] 8 Genesis 24-25
[_] 9 Genesis 26-28
[_] 10 Genesis 29-30
[_] 11 Genesis 31-32
[_] 12 Genesis 33-35
[_] 13 Genesis 36-38
[_] 14 Genesis 39-41
[_] 15 Genesis 42-44
[_] 16 Genesis 45-47
[_] 17 Genesis 48-50
[_] 18 Exodus 1-3
[_] 19 Exodus 4-6
[_] 20 Exodus 7-9
[_] 21 Exodus 10-12
[_] 22 Exodus 13-15
[_] 23 Exodus 16-18
[_] 24 Exodus 19-21
[_] 25 Exodus 22-24
[_] 26 Exodus 25-27
[_] 27 Exodus 28-29
[_] 28 Exodus 30-32
[_] 29 Exodus 33-35
[_] 30 Exodus 36-38
[_] 31 Exodus 39-40

FEBRUARY

[_] 1 Leviticus 1-4
[_] 2 Leviticus 5-7
[_] 3 Leviticus 8-9
[_] 4 Leviticus 10-12
[_] 5 Leviticus 13
[_] 6 Leviticus 14-15
[_] 7 Leviticus 16-18
[_] 8 Leviticus 19-21
[_] 9 Leviticus 22-23
[_] 10 Leviticus 24-25
[_] 11 Leviticus 26-27
[_] 12 Numbers 1-2
[_] 13 Numbers 3-4
[_] 14 Numbers 5-6
[_] 15 Numbers 7
[_] 16 Numbers 8-10
[_] 17 Numbers 11-13
[_] 18 Numbers 14-15
[_] 19 Numbers 16-18
[_] 20 Numbers 19-21
[_] 21 Numbers 22-24
[_] 22 Numbers 25-26
[_] 23 Numbers 27-29
[_] 24 Numbers 30-31
[_] 25 Numbers 32-33
[_] 26 Numbers 34-36
[_] 27 Deuteronomy 1-2
[_] 28 Deuteronomy 3-4

MARCH

[_] 1 Deuteronomy 5-7
[_] 2 Deuteronomy 8-10
[_] 3 Deuteronomy 11-13
[_] 4 Deuteronomy 14-17
[_] 5 Deuteronomy 18-20
[_] 6 Deuteronomy 21-23
[_] 7 Deuteronomy 24-26
[_] 8 Deuteronomy 27-28
[_] 9 Deuteronomy 29-31
[_] 10 Deuteronomy 32-34
[_] 11 Joshua 1-4
[_] 12 Joshua 5-7
[_] 13 Joshua 8-9
[_] 14 Joshua 10-11
[_] 15 Joshua 12-14
[_] 16 Joshua 15-17
[_] 17 Joshua 18-20
[_] 18 Joshua 21-22
[_] 19 Joshua 23-24
[_] 20 Judges 1-3
[_] 21 Judges 4-6
[_] 22 Judges 7-8
[_] 23 Judges 9-10
[_] 24 Judges 11-13
[_] 25 Judges 14-16
[_] 26 Judges 17-19
[_] 27 Judges 20-21
[_] 28 Ruth 1-4
[_] 29 1 Samuel 1-3
[_] 30 1 Samuel 4-7
[_] 31 1 Samuel 8-10

APRIL

[_] 1 1 Samuel 11-13
[_] 2 1 Samuel 14-15
[_] 3 1 Samuel 16-17
[_] 4 1 Samuel 18-20
[_] 5 1 Samuel 21-24
[_] 6 1 Samuel 25-27
[_] 7 1 Samuel 28-31
[_] 8 2 Samuel 1-3
[_] 9 2 Samuel 4-7
[_] 10 2 Samuel 8-11
[_] 11 2 Samuel 12-13
[_] 12 2 Samuel 14-15
[_] 13 2 Samuel 16-17
[_] 14 2 Samuel 18-19
[_] 15 2 Samuel 20-22
[_] 16 2 Samuel 23-24
[_] 17 1 Kings 1
[_] 18 1 Kings 2-3
[_] 19 1 Kings 4-6
[_] 20 1 Kings 7
[_] 21 1 Kings 8
[_] 22 1 Kings 9-10
[_] 23 1 Kings 11-12
[_] 24 1 Kings 13-14
[_] 25 1 Kings 15-17
[_] 26 1 Kings 18-19
[_] 27 1 Kings 20-22
[_] 28 2 Kings 1-2
[_] 29 2 Kings 3-4
[_] 30 2 Kings 5-7

MAY

[_] 1 2 Kings 8-9
[_] 2 2 Kings 10-12
[_] 3 2 Kings 13-14
[_] 4 2 Kings 15-16
[_] 5 2 Kings 17-18
[_] 6 2 Kings 19-21
[_] 7 2 Kings 22-25
[_] 8 1 Chronicles 1
[_] 9 1 Chronicles 2-4
[_] 10 1 Chronicles 5-6
[_] 11 1 Chronicles 7-9
[_] 12 1 Chronicles 10-12
[_] 13 1 Chronicles 13-16
[_] 14 1 Chronicles 17-19
[_] 15 1 Chronicles 20-23
[_] 16 1 Chronicles 24-26
[_] 17 1 Chronicles 27-29
[_] 18 2 Chronicles 1-4
[_] 19 2 Chronicles 5-7
[_] 20 2 Chronicles 8-10
[_] 21 2 Chronicles 11-14
[_] 22 2 Chronicles 15-18
[_] 23 2 Chronicles 19-22
[_] 24 2 Chronicles 23-25
[_] 25 2 Chronicles 26-28
[_] 26 2 Chronicles 29-30
[_] 27 2 Chronicles 31-33
[_] 28 2 Chronicles 34-36
[_] 29 Ezra 1-2
[_] 30 Ezra 3-5
[_] 31 Ezra 6-8

JUNE

[_] 1 Ezra 9-10
[_] 2 Nehemiah 1-3
[_] 3 Nehemiah 4-6
[_] 4 Nehemiah 7-8
[_] 5 Nehemiah 9-10
[_] 6 Nehemiah 11-13
[_] 7 Esther 1-3
[_] 8 Esther 4-7
[_] 9 Esther 8-10
[_] 10 Job 1-5
[_] 11 Job 6-10
[_] 12 Job 11-15
[_] 13 Job 16-21
[_] 14 Job 22-28
[_] 15 Job 29-33
[_] 16 Job 34-37
[_] 17 Job 38-42
[_] 18 Psalms 1-9
[_] 19 Psalms 10-17
[_] 20 Psalms 18-22
[_] 21 Psalms 23-31
[_] 22 Psalms 32-37
[_] 23 Psalms 38-44
[_] 24 Psalms 45-51
[_] 25 Psalms 52-59
[_] 26 Psalms 60-67
[_] 27 Psalms 68-71
[_] 28 Psalms 72-77
[_] 29 Psalms 78-81
[_] 30 Psalms 82-89

JULY

[_] 1 Psalms 90-97
[_] 2 Psalms 98-104
[_] 3 Psalms 105-107
[_] 4 Psalms 108-116
[_] 5 Psalms 117-118
[_] 6 Psalm 119
[_] 7 Psalms 120-135
[_] 8 Psalms 136-142
[_] 9 Psalms 143-150
[_] 10 Proverbs 1-4
[_] 11 Proverbs 5-8
[_] 12 Proverbs 9-13
[_] 13 Proverbs 14-17
[_] 14 Proverbs 18-21
[_] 15 Proverbs 22-24
[_] 16 Proverbs 25-28
[_] 17 Proverbs 29-31
[_] 18 Ecclesiastes 1-6
[_] 19 Ecclesiastes 7-12
[_] 20 Song of Solomon 1-8
[_] 21 Isaiah 1-4
[_] 22 Isaiah 5-8
[_] 23 Isaiah 9-12
[_] 24 Isaiah 13-16
[_] 25 Isaiah 17-21
[_] 26 Isaiah 22-25
[_] 27 Isaiah 26-28
[_] 28 Isaiah 29-31
[_] 29 Isaiah 32-35
[_] 30 Isaiah 36-38
[_] 31 Isaiah 39-42

AUGUST

[_] 1 Isaiah 43-47
[_] 2 Isaiah 48-51
[_] 3 Isaiah 52-56
[_] 4 Isaiah 57-59
[_] 5 Isaiah 60-63
[_] 6 Isaiah 64-66
[_] 7 Jeremiah 1-3
[_] 8 Jeremiah 4-6
[_] 9 Jeremiah 7-9
[_] 10 Jeremiah 10-12
[_] 11 Jeremiah 13-15
[_] 12 Jeremiah 16-18
[_] 13 Jeremiah 19-22
[_] 14 Jeremiah 23-25
[_] 15 Jeremiah 26-27
[_] 16 Jeremiah 28-30
[_] 17 Jeremiah 31-32
[_] 18 Jeremiah 33-35
[_] 19 Jeremiah 36-38
[_] 20 Jeremiah 39-41
[_] 21 Jeremiah 42-44
[_] 22 Jeremiah 45-48
[_] 23 Jeremiah 49-50
[_] 24 Jeremiah 51-52
[_] 25 Lamentations 1-2
[_] 26 Lamentations 3-5
[_] 27 Ezekiel 1-4
[_] 28 Ezekiel 5-8
[_] 29 Ezekiel 9-12
[_] 30 Ezekiel 13-15
[_] 31 Ezekiel 16

SEPTEMBER

[_] 1 Ezekiel 17-19
[_] 2 Ezekiel 20-21
[_] 3 Ezekiel 22-23
[_] 4 Ezekiel 24-26
[_] 5 Ezekiel 27-28
[_] 6 Ezekiel 29-31
[_] 7 Ezekiel 32-33
[_] 8 Ezekiel 34-36
[_] 9 Ezekiel 37-38
[_] 10 Ezekiel 39-40
[_] 11 Ezekiel 41-43
[_] 12 Ezekiel 44-45
[_] 13 Ezekiel 46-48
[_] 14 Daniel 1-2
[_] 15 Daniel 3-4
[_] 16 Daniel 5-6
[_] 17 Daniel 7-8
[_] 18 Daniel 9-10
[_] 19 Daniel 11-12
[_] 20 Hosea 1-7
[_] 21 Hosea 8-14
[_] 22 Joel 1-3
[_] 23 Amos 1-5
[_] 24 Amos 6-9/Obadiah
[_] 25 Jonah 1-4/
Micah 1-2
[_] 26 Micah 3-7
[_] 27 Nahum/Habakkuk
[_] 28 Zephaniah/Haggai
[_] 29 Zechariah 1-6
[_] 30 Zechariah 7-10

OCTOBER

[_] 1 Zechariah 11-14
[_] 2 Malachi 1-4
[_] 3 Matthew 1-4
[_] 4 Matthew 5-6
[_] 5 Matthew 7-9
[_] 6 Matthew 10-12
[_] 7 Matthew 13-14
[_] 8 Matthew 15-17
[_] 9 Matthew 18-20
[_] 10 Matthew 21-22
[_] 11 Matthew 23-24
[_] 12 Matthew 25-26
[_] 13 Matthew 27-28
[_] 14 Mark 1-3
[_] 15 Mark 4-5
[_] 16 Mark 6-7
[_] 17 Mark 8-9
[_] 18 Mark 10-11
[_] 19 Mark 12-13
[_] 20 Mark 14-16
[_] 21 Luke 1
[_] 22 Luke 2-3
[_] 23 Luke 4-5
[_] 24 Luke 6-7
[_] 25 Luke 8
[_] 26 Luke 9
[_] 27 Luke 10-11
[_] 28 Luke 12-13
[_] 29 Luke 14-16
[_] 30 Luke 17-18
[_] 31 Luke 19-20

NOVEMBER

[_] 1 Luke 21-22
[_] 2 Luke 23-24
[_] 3 John 1-3
[_] 4 John 4-5
[_] 5 John 6-7
[_] 6 John 8-9
[_] 7 John 10-11
[_] 8 John 12-13
[_] 9 John 14-16
[_] 10 John 17-18
[_] 11 John 19-21
[_] 12 Acts 1-3
[_] 13 Acts 4-6
[_] 14 Acts 7-8
[_] 15 Acts 9-10
[_] 16 Acts 11-13
[_] 17 Acts 14-16
[_] 18 Acts 17-18
[_] 19 Acts 19-20
[_] 20 Acts 21-22
[_] 21 Acts 23-25
[_] 22 Acts 26-28
[_] 23 Romans 1-3
[_] 24 Romans 4-7
[_] 25 Romans 8-10
[_] 26 Romans 11-14
[_] 27 Romans 15-16
[_] 28 1 Corinthians 1-4
[_] 29 1 Corinthians 5-8
[_] 30 1 Corinthians 9-11

DECEMBER

[_] 1 1 Corinthians 12-14
[_] 2 1 Corinthians 15-16
[_] 3 2 Corinthians 1-4
[_] 4 2 Corinthians 5-8
[_] 5 2 Corinthians 9-13
[_] 6 Galatians 1-6
[_] 7 Ephesians 1-3
[_] 8 Ephesians 4-6
[_] 9 Philippians 1-4
[_] 10 Colossians 1-4
[_] 11 1 Thessalonians 1-5
[_] 12 2 Thessalonians 1-3
[_] 13 1 Timothy 1-4
[_] 14 1 Timothy 5-6
[_] 15 2 Timothy 1-4
[_] 16 Titus/Philemon
[_] 17 Hebrews 1-5
[_] 18 Hebrews 6-9
[_] 19 Hebrews 10-11
[_] 20 Hebrews 12-13
[_] 21 James 1-5
[_] 22 1 Peter 1-5
[_] 23 2 Peter 1-3
[_] 24 1 John 1-5
[_] 25 2, 3 John, Jude
[_] 26 Revelation 1-3
[_] 27 Revelation 4-8
[_] 28 Revelation 9-12
[_] 29 Revelation 13-16
[_] 30 Revelation 17-19
[_] 31 Revelation 20-22

Appendix 3

A Starter Schedule For A New Believer

[_] 1 John 1:1-28*
[_] 2 John 1:29-51
[_] 3 John 2:1-25
[_] 4 John 3:1-21
[_] 5 John 3:22-36
[_] 6 John 4:1-26*
[_] 7 John 4:27-54
[_] 8 John 5:1-30
[_] 9 John 5:31-6:13*
[_] 10 John 6:14-40*
[_] 11 John 6:41-71
[_] 12 John 7:1-24*
[_] 13 John 7:25-52
[_] 14 John 7:53-8:20
[_] 15 John 8:21-38*
[_] 16 John 8:39-59
[_] 17 John 9:1-23*
[_] 18 John 9:24-41*
[_] 19 John 10:1-21
[_] 20 John 10:22-42
[_] 21 John 11:1-29*
[_] 22 John 11:30-53
[_] 23 John 11:54-12:19
[_] 24 John 12:20-36a
[_] 25 John 12:36b-50*
[_] 26 John 13:1-30
[_] 27 John 13:31-14:14
[_] 28 John 14:15-31
[_] 29 John 15:1-27*
[_] 30 John 16:1-16*
[_] 31 John 16:17-33
[_] 32 John 17:1-26
[_] 33 John 18:1-27
[_] 34 John 18:28-40
[_] 35 John 19:1-22
[_] 36 John 19:23-42
[_] 37 John 20:1-23
[_] 38 John 20:24--21:14
[_] 39 John 21:15-2